D1242985

THE PENNINE WAY

About the Author

Paddy Dillon is a prolific walker and guidebook writer, with over 40 books to his name and contributions to 25 other books. He has written extensively for several outdoor magazines and other publications and has appeared on radio and television.

Paddy was born and reared close to the Pennine Way, and incorporated parts of the route into his earliest forays into the Pennines. He has walked the entire Pennine Way three times and has covered many parts of the route on dozens of occasions, throughout the seasons, in all kinds of weather. Paddy has decades of experience of the Pennine Way, and in this guide he offers information and encouragement to others who wish to follow this popular, long-established trail. Paddy uses a palmtop computer to write his route descriptions while walking. His descriptions are therefore precise, having been written at the very point at which the reader uses them.

Paddy is an indefatigable long-distance walker who has walked all of Britain's National Trails and several major European trails. He lives on the fringes of the English Lake District and has walked, and written about walking, in every county throughout the British Isles. He has led guided walking holidays and has walked throughout Europe, as well as in Nepal, Tibet, and the Rocky Mountains of Canada and the US. Paddy is a member of the Outdoor Writers and Photographers Guild.

Other Cicerone guides by the author

GR20 – Corsica
Irish Coastal Walks
The Cleveland Way and the
    Yorkshire Wolds Way
The GR5 Trail
The Great Glen Way
The Irish Coast to Coast Walk
The Mountains of Ireland
The National Trails
The North York Moors
The Reivers Way
The South West Coast Path

The Teesdale Way
Trekking through Mallorca
Walking in County Durham
Walking in Madeira
Walking in Malta
Walking in the Canary Islands –
    East & West
Walking in the Isles of Scilly
Walking in the North Pennines
Walking on the Isle of Arran
Walking the Galloway Hills

THE PENNINE WAY

by

Paddy Dillon

CICERONE

2 POLICE SQUARE, MILNTHORPE, CUMBRIA LA7 7PY
www.cicerone.co.uk

Third edition © Paddy Dillon 2010
ISBN: 978 1 85284 575 9
Previous editions © Martin Collins 1998, 2003
ISBN-10: 1 85284 386 1

Printed by MCC Graphics, Spain

A catalogue record for this book is available from the British Library.

All photographs are by the author.

OS **Ordnance Survey®** This product includes mapping data licenses from Ordnance Survey® with the permission of the Controller of Her Majesty's Stationery Office. © Crown copyright 2010. All rights reserved. Licence number PU100012932.

Advice to Readers

Readers are advised that, while every effort is made by our authors to ensure the accuracy of guidebooks as they go to print, changes can occur during the lifetime of an edition. Please check the Cicerone website (www.cicerone.co.uk) for any updates before planning your trip. It is also advisable to check information on such things as transport, accommodation and shops locally. Even rights of way can be altered over time. We are always grateful for information about any discrepancies between a guidebook and the facts on the ground, sent by email to info@cicerone.co.uk or by post to Cicerone, 2 Police Square, Milnthorpe LA7 7PY, United Kingdom.

Front cover: *Looking across Blackton Reservoir in Baldersdale, from the moorland flanks of Goldsborough (Day 11)*

CONTENTS

Warning

Mountain walking can be a dangerous activity carrying a risk of personal injury or death. It should be undertaken only by those with a full understanding of the risks and with the training and experience to evaluate them. While every care and effort has been taken in the preparation of this guide, the user should be aware that conditions can be highly variable and can change quickly, materially affecting the seriousness of a mountain walk. Therefore, except for any liability which cannot be excluded by law, neither Cicerone nor the author accept liability for damage of any nature (including damage to property, personal injury or death) arising directly or indirectly from the information in this book.

To call out the Mountain Rescue, ring 999 or the European emergency number 112: this will connect you via any available network. Once connected to the emergency operator, ask for the police.

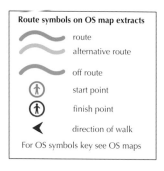

Route symbols on OS map extracts

route

alternative route

off route

start point

finish point

direction of walk

For OS symbols key see OS maps

The distinctive profile of Pen-y-Ghent as seen across a limestone pavement near Dale Head (Day 7)

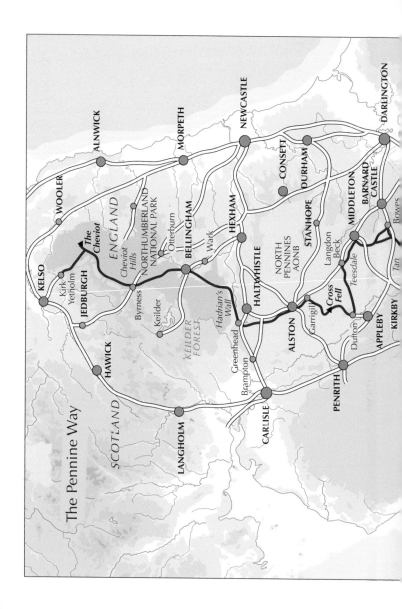

The Pennine Way

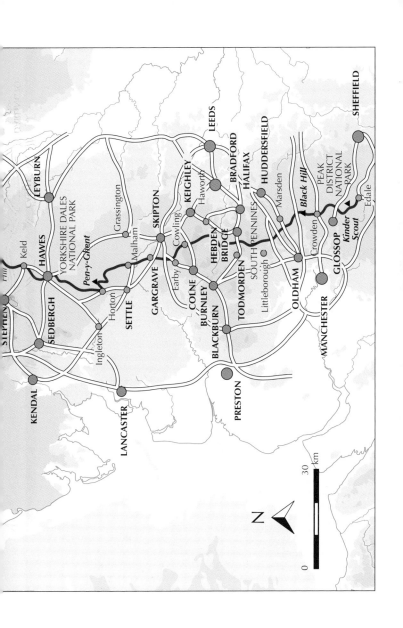

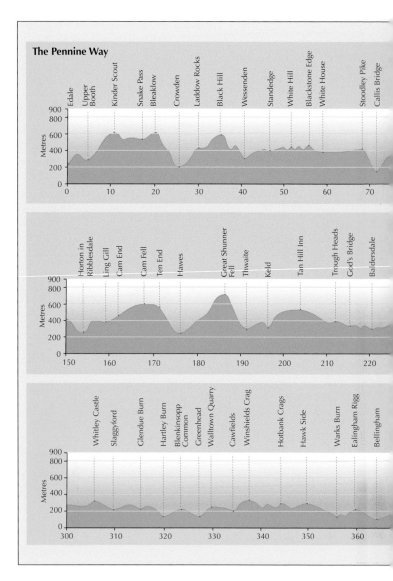

The Pennine Way

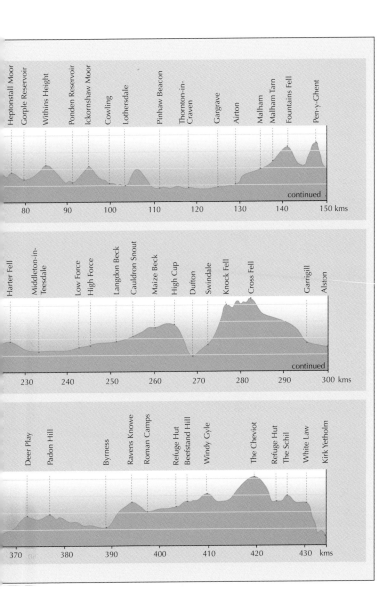

Top profile (80–150 kms):

Heptonstall Moor · Gorple Reservoir · Withins Height · Ponden Reservoir · Ickornshaw Moor · Cowling · Lothersdale · Pinhaw Beacon · Thornton-in-Craven · Gargrave · Airton · Malham · Malham Tarn · Fountains Fell · Pen-y-Ghent

continued

80   90   100   110   120   130   140   150 kms

Middle profile (230–300 kms):

Harter Fell · Middleton-in-Teesdale · Low Force · High Force · Langdon Beck · Cauldron Snout · Maize Beck · High Cup · Dufton · Swindale · Knock Fell · Cross Fell · Garrigill · Alston

continued

230   240   250   260   270   280   290   300 kms

Bottom profile (370–430 kms):

Deer Play · Padon Hill · Byrness · Ravens Knowe · Roman Camps · Refuge Hut · Beefstand Hill · Windy Gyle · The Cheviot · Refuge Hut · The Schil · White Law · Kirk Yetholm

370   380   390   400   410   420   430 kms

Beck Hall, a café and bed and breakfast beside the River Aire in the village of Malham (Day 6)

PREFACE

Of all the many guidebooks I have written this one is the most personal. The Pennine Way is intricately bound up with my family history. I was born and raised only 6 miles from the Pennine Way and the route was opened when I was only seven years old. My family included some staunch walkers who used to talk about it from time to time. One of them went and walked it, returning with tales to inspire others. As young teenagers, a friend and I stumbled across a Pennine Way signpost on the moors and wondered how long it might take us to walk to Scotland. Soon afterwards, a chance copy of Alfred Wainwright's *Pennine Way Companion*, laid it all out for me in black and white.

I could have walked the Pennine Way at the age of 16, but I chose to follow it northwards only as far as Cross Fell, then making a beeline for the Lake District, exploring for a week and walking home via the Yorkshire Dales. I finally walked the whole route for the first time when I was 21, and it snowed for the first five days!

Throughout the 1970s, if you told anyone you were a keen walker, they would ask, 'And have you walked the Pennine Way?' And anyone actually walking the route might have been asked, 'Are you walking the Pennine Way, or just walking for pleasure?', as if the two were mutually exclusive! The route was regarded, rightly or wrongly, as something that every 'proper' walker should aspire to, generating something of a backlash, with some people vowing never to set foot on it.

One thing became painfully obvious throughout the 1970s: the Pennine Way was being trodden to death. Although I always enjoyed walking parts of the route, it was distinctly unpleasant to wade through the mud, occasionally plumbing waist-deep bogs, where the peat had been trodden into the consistency of cold, black porridge. Apart from occasional forays during the 1980s, I left the route well alone while the problems of over-use and erosion were addressed, ultimately by completely rebuilding several stretches of the trail.

Once everything had bedded down and grassed over I renewed my acquaintance. It was worth the wait, and as the years roll by, the stone-paved paths will become as much a part of the Pennine Way as the centuries-old packhorse 'causeys' that preceded it. The scenery remains the same as ever and only the conditions immediately underfoot have changed, and for the better.

Sadly, the Pennine Way is no longer held in the high regard it enjoyed at the outset. Today's walkers have other National Trails to choose and infinite opportunities to walk challenging trails abroad. This is well and good, but the Pennine Way remains the toughest of the National Trails, one that every long-distance walker should aspire to. Long may it enjoy a future as part of Britain's outdoor heritage.

Paddy Dillon, 2010

Slightly off-route, the view from the edge of Malham Cove after crossing the limestone pavement on top (Day 7)

INTRODUCTION

WANTED: A LONG GREEN TRAIL

You could say it all started on 22 June 1935. An article appeared in the *Daily Herald* newspaper entitled 'Wanted: A Long Green Trail', written by the ramblers' champion Tom Stephenson. 'Why should we not press for something akin to the Appalachian Trail?' he asked. 'A Pennine Way from the Peak to the Cheviots.' He imagined that the route would be 'a faint line on the Ordnance Maps which the feet of grateful pilgrims would, with the passing years, engrave on the face of the land.' Well, the engraving went rather deep in places, even to the extent that you could claim the route was carved in stone, but that is only a testimony to its popularity.

It took 30 years of lobbying and hard work to steer the Pennine Way to its official opening in April 1965. As a long-distance walk it is impressive, stretching from Edale in the Peak District National Park onto the gritstone moors of the South Pennines. The way passes through the verdant Yorkshire Dales National Park, then

The official start is the Old Nags Head in the village of Edale (Day 1)

The official end is the Border Hotel in the village of Kirk Yetholm (Day 20)

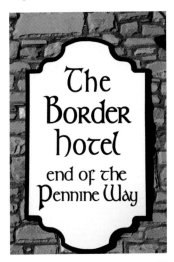

crosses the bleak and remote North Pennines. Not content to finish there, it then traverses Hadrian's Wall and runs through the Northumberland National Park. High in the Cheviot Hills, it finally steps over the border into Scotland to finish at Kirk Yetholm. It measures over 435km (270 miles), involving a cumulative ascent of 11,225m (36,825ft). Most walkers take between two and three weeks to cover the distance, and there are many ways to create a schedule to suit people's different expectations.

PENNINE GEOLOGY

As a teenager I was not content simply to admire the Pennines. I wielded a hammer and chisel so that I could take great chunks of them home with me!

Pennine geology is relatively easy to understand, although in a few places it becomes very complex. The oldest bedrock is seldom seen on the Pennine Way, revealing itself only around Malham and Dufton. Ancient Silurian slate at Malham Tarn, along with Ordovician mudstone and volcanic rock above Dufton, date back 450 million years. These rocks are revealed only where fault lines bring them to the surface. The Weardale Granite, which underlies the North Pennines, outcrops nowhere and was only 'proved' by a borehole sunk at Rookhope in 1961.

In the Devonian period, around 395 million years ago, violent volcanic activity laid the foundations of the

Cheviot Hills, at the northern end of the Pennine Way. All the lower hills are made of andesite lavas, while the central parts are formed of a massive dome of granite, pushed into the Earth's crust some 360 million years ago and only recently exposed to the elements.

During the Carboniferous period, around 350 to 300 million years ago, the whole region was covered by a warm, shallow, tropical sea. Countless billions of shelled, soft-bodied creatures lived and died in this sea. Coral reefs grew, and even microscopic organisms often had hard external or internal structures. Over the aeons, these creatures left their hard shells in heaps on the seabed, and these deposits became the massive grey limestones seen to best effect in the Yorkshire Dales today.

Even while thick beds of limestone were being laid down, storms were eroding distant mountain ranges. Vast rivers brought mud, sand and gravel down into the sea. These murky deposits reduced the amount of light entering the water, causing delicate coral reefs and other creatures to perish. As more mud and sand was washed into the sea, a vast delta spread across the region.

At times, shoals of sand and gravel stood above the waterline, and these became colonised by strange, fern-like trees. The level of water in the rivers and sea was in a state of flux. Sometimes the delta was completely flooded, so the plants would be buried

Dimpled grooves in a streambed on Black Hill Moss are the fossilised remains of ancient tree-ferns (Day 9)

under more sand and gravel. The compressed plant material within the beds of sand and mud became thin bands of coal, known as the Coal Measures. This alternating series of sandstones and mudstones, with occasional seams of coal, can be seen best in the Dark Peak and the South Pennines. Remnants of the series can also be studied on the higher summits of the Yorkshire Dales and North Pennines.

The Carboniferous rocks were laid down in layers, helping to explain what happened next, around 295 million years ago. An extensive mass of molten dolerite was squeezed, under enormous pressure, between the layers of rock – rather like jam between two slices of bread. This rock is always prominent wherever it outcrops, and is referred to as the Whin Sill.

Almost 300 million years are 'missing' from the Pennine geological record, in which time the range has been broken into enormous blocks by faulting. The Yorkshire Dales and North Pennines display plenty of limestone, as their 'blocks' stand higher than the Peak District and South Pennines. The entire range was scoured by glaciers during the Ice Age, and many parts are covered with glacial detritus in the form of boulder clay, sand and gravel. More recent climatic changes resulted in the upland soil becoming so waterlogged that thick deposits of peat have formed on most of the higher moorlands.

PENNINE SCENERY

The underlying geology of the Pennines shapes the scenery along the Pennine Way. The Dark Peak and the South Pennines, whose foundations are sandstones and shales, with gritstone 'edges', give rise to acid clay soils, which encourages the formation of thick blanket bog. This bog has been growing for the past 7000

Massive Carboniferous limestone pavement displays clints and grikes above Malham Cove (Day 6)

The Pennine Way is no longer routed over the fragile blanket bogs of the Kinder Scout plateau

years, but in many places it is decaying, so that the moorlands are riven by peat channels, or 'groughs', with high banks of peat between them, known as 'hags'. Given that the blanket bogs represent an enormous carbon 'sink', their rapid decay gives cause for concern and efforts are being made to stabilise the remaining bogs and reverse the trend.

Where limestone dominates, particularly in the Yorkshire Dales but also in parts of the North Pennines, the landscape often looks fresh and green, covered in short, dense, sheep-grazed turf, with bright cliffs and outcrops, or 'scars', of limestone poking through. Limestone country is fascinating, mostly because of the way the rock dissolves slowly over the aeons, giving rise to a distinctive landscape known as 'karst' topography.

Limestone doesn't just wear down like other rocks but dissolves inside itself, becoming riddled with caves and passages. When these are close to the surface, they may collapse, forming 'shake holes'.

In the North Pennines, the existence of the igneous Whin Sill, sandwiched between older beds of rock, forms some of the most striking landscapes in the North Pennines and Northumberland. The Teesdale waterfalls, High Cup and the rugged crest bearing Hadrian's Wall are all formed by the Whin Sill, which also outcrops on the Northumberland coast.

Technically, and geologically, the Pennines end just south of Hadrian's Wall, so the continuation northwards through Northumberland results in another shift in the scenery. While Carboniferous rocks lie underfoot at

Despite the Pennine Way being a popular trail, some paths along the route do become overgrown

Descending from Auchope Cairn towards the mountain refuge hut above Hen Hole (Day 20)

first, by the time the high Cheviot Hills are reached, the bedrock is either lava or granite. The central granite mass of The Cheviot stands broad-shouldered, with all the other Cheviot Hills huddled around it. The poor acid soil supports thick blanket bog. Many walkers, seeing the Cheviot Hills after spending so long in the Pennines, are surprised at how hilly they are, but this is short-lived, as the Pennine Way ends suddenly with a descent into rolling, pastoral countryside.

THE HELM WIND

Most walkers on the Pennine Way hear about the 'Helm Wind' but few understand what it is. The Helm Wind is the only wind in Britain with a name. It only blows from one direction and

it gives rise to a peculiar set of conditions. Other winds blow from all points of the compass, but the Helm is very strictly defined, restricted to the East Fellside flank of the North Pennines, and according to local lore, no matter how much it rages, it cannot cross the Eden.

First, there needs to be a north-easterly wind, with a minimum speed of 25kph (15mph), which the Beaufort Scale calls a 'moderate breeze'. This isn't the prevailing wind direction and it tends to occur in the winter and spring. Track the air mass from the North Sea, across low-lying country, as far as the Tyne Gap. The air gets pushed over Hexhamshire Common, crossing moorlands at around 300m (1000ft). It next crosses moorlands at around 600m (2000ft) and then Cross

The Helm Wind blows down the steep western slopes of the North Pennines

Fell and its neighbours are reached at almost 900m (3000ft). There are no low-lying gaps across the North Pennines, so there is nowhere for the air mass to go but over the top.

As the air is pushed up from sea level, it cools considerably. Any moisture it picked up from the sea condenses to form clouds, and these are most noticeable as they build up above the East Fellside. This feature is known as the 'Helm Cap'. If there is little moisture present it is white, while greater moisture content makes it much darker, resulting in rainfall. Bear in mind at this point that the air mass is not only cooler, but as a result it is also denser than the air mass sitting in the Vale of Eden.

After crossing the highest parts of the North Pennines, the north-easterly wind is cold, dense, and

suddenly runs out of high ground. The air literally 'falls' down the East Fellside slope, and if it could be seen, it would probably look like a tidal wave. This, and only this, is the Helm Wind. The greater the north-easterly wind speed, the greater the force with which it plummets down the East Fellside, and if it is particularly strong, wet and cold, it is capable of great damage. Very few habitations have ever been built on this slope, and the villages below were generally built with their backs to the East Fellside.

The air mass now does some peculiar things, having dropped, cold and dense, to hit a relatively warm air mass sitting in the Vale of Eden. A 'wave' of air literally rises up and curls back on itself. As warm and cold air mix, there is another phase of condensation inside an aerial vortex, resulting in the formation of a thin, twisting band of cloud that seems to hover mid-air, no matter how hard the wind blows at ground level. This cloud is called the 'Helm Bar' and is conclusive proof that the Helm Wind is 'on', as the locals say.

Local folk say that no matter how hard the Helm Wind blows, it can never cross the Eden. All the wind's energy is expended in aerial acrobatics on the East Fellside, where it can roar and rumble for several days, while the Vale of Eden experiences only gentle surface winds. North-easterly winds are uncommon and short-lived, so after only a few days the system breaks down and the usual blustery south-westerly winds are restored. In the meantime, don't refer to any old wind as the Helm Wind until all its characteristics have been noted, including the north-east wind, the Helm Cap and the Helm Bar.

An increasingly rare species - the native British white-clawed crayfish in the Yorkshire Dales

A well camouflaged adder on a heather moor adopts its strike position when approached too closely

WILDLIFE

Pennine pastures offer good grazing for sheep and cattle, while the higher moorlands offer passable grazing for sheep in the summer months. Only in the North Pennines are fell ponies likely to be seen, and feral goats are occasionally spotted in the Cheviot Hills. Other mammals that can be seen include foxes, badgers, hares and rabbits, along with small rodents. The heather moorlands of the Pennines are managed for grouse-shooting, which involves the control of 'vermin', meaning anything likely to affect the numbers of grouse on the moors. Red grouse are dominant, but there are small areas in the North Pennines with black grouse too. The

23

plaintive piping of the curlew will be heard on the moors, while snipe may be flushed from cover. Lapwings are notable in high pastures, usually when trying to distract walkers from their nesting sites. The reservoirs and bog pools attract all manner of wildfowl and waders, and it is not uncommon to find raucous colonies of gulls breeding on the high moors, far from the sea. Reptiles include common lizards, adders and grass snakes, although these are rarely seen. Amphibians include frogs and increasingly rare newts. Emperor moths are notable on the high moors, while the native white-clawed crayfish is under great threat from competition and disease introduced by non-native species.

PLANT LIFE

For the most part, the high Pennines feature tussocky moor grass with boggy patches of sphagnum moss. In the summer months, vast areas of nodding bog cotton give the impression of snow-covered slopes. There is rather less heather than most people expect,

Top *Bog cotton thrives on wet, boggy, acid peat moorlands where other plants would struggle*

Middle *Cloudberries, arctic remnant plants, only grow on the highest and bleakest parts of the Pennine Way*

Bottom *Juniper is relatively rare in the wild, but is abundant in parts of Upper Teesdale (Days 12 and 13)*

and much of it has been managed to provide a habitat for red grouse. The dominant species is ling, although there are occasional areas of bell heather. Heather is burnt on a rotational basis, so that there are always young heather shoots for grouse to feed on, as well as denser 'leggy' heather for shelter. Heather seeds are fairly resistant to fire, but in places where heather is over-burnt, invasive bracken is quick to take hold. Some heather moorlands also feature bilberry and crowberry, while the higher, bleaker, boggier moorlands are home to an arctic remnant – cloudberry.

There is very little tillage on Pennine farms, and most fields are managed as pastures for farm stock. Some fields are managed for hay, and in the dale-heads of the North Pennines, haymaking comes so late in the summer that wild flowers have a chance to drop their seeds, making the meadows rich in species.

The range of plants thriving in Upper Teesdale owes its existence to several factors. Arctic/alpine species survive because the climate in this bleak region suits them, keeping taller and more competitive plants at bay. The underlying crumbling 'sugar limestone' suits some species, while others grow on sodden, acid peat bogs. Plants that once grew in well-wooded areas now survive by adapting to life in the shade of boulders and cliffs. Many people have heard of the spring gentian, which is strikingly blue on sunny days in early summer, but few

know where to find it. Other species of note include the mountain pansy, alpine bistort, bird's eye primrose, Teesdale violet and blue moor grass. These grow alongside more commonplace wild thyme, tormentil, thrift and harebells, while wood anemones and woodland ferns have adapted to non-wooded habitats. The 'Teesdale Assemblage' of plants are survivors from bygone ages, reminding visitors how habitats have changed over time.

NATIONAL PARKS

The Pennine Way traverses three National Parks and one Area of Outstanding Natural Beauty. In fact, the route could be broken down into five unequal stages according to the type of area it crosses.

Only the northern part of the Peak District National Park, the Dark Peak, is on the route. It is characterised by broad, bleak, high-altitude moorland. The Peak District only features for the first two days of walking, to Standedge, then gives way to the gentler South Pennines. While this isn't a National Park, it does have a distinct identity as far northwards as the Aire Gap, taking two or three days to cover. The Yorkshire Dales National Park captures the attention of Wayfarers for four or five days, from Gargrave to the Tan Hill Inn. Next comes the enormous North Pennines Area of Outstanding Natural Beauty, which for reasons unknown was never given National Park status, despite being one of the

A flagstone path climbs through fields above Edale before descending to Upper Booth (Day 1)

wildest upland areas of England. It is home to enormous National Nature Reserves and claims to be the most scientifically studied upland region in the world. Crossing this AONB on the Pennine Way takes five or six days. Then, when the Pennines peter out at the Tyne Gap, the route enters the Northumberland National Park, stretching from Hadrian's Wall to the Cheviot Hills and taking a final four or five days to traverse.

TRAVEL TO AND FROM THE PENNINE WAY

By air

For overseas visitors, the handiest access for the start of the Pennine Way is Manchester Airport, served by flights from around the world. Catch a train from the airport to Manchester Piccadilly and change for Edale and the start of the Pennine Way. Leaving the northern end of the route isn't as simple, requiring careful study of local bus and train timetables, but the airports at Edinburgh and Newcastle can be reached for homeward flights.

By rail

Regular daily Northern Trains serve Edale from Manchester and Sheffield (www.northernrail.org). Trains cross the Pennine Way only in a few places, notably Hebden Bridge, Gargrave and Horton in Ribblesdale. Greenhead no longer has a station, the nearest being off-route at Haltwhistle. There are no railways near Kirk Yetholm, so if you are intending to travel home by

The broad top of Cross Fell has only a vague path and care needs to be taken to locate the descent (Day 14)

rail, you will need to catch a bus to Berwick-upon-Tweed or Edinburgh.

By bus

There are several local bus routes crossing the Pennine Way. Where useful buses exist, either connecting with other parts of the route, or leading off-route to nearby towns and villages, there is a brief mention of them in the text. For fuller details, obtain the free 'Pennine Way Accommodation and Public Transport Guide' available from tourist information offices, or from www.nationaltrail.co.uk/pennineway. To check details of buses in advance, a useful website is www.traveline.org.uk. While you are walking the route, Traveline can be contacted on 0871 2002233. Always ensure that you obtain up-to-date bus times a day or two before you need them, as some services are very sparse.

WHEN TO WALK

The Pennine Way is naturally busiest in the summer months, when most people take their longest holiday of the year. This is a fine time to walk, as all facilities and services are available, and the weather is generally warm and sunny, with plenty of daylight hours. In August, when the heather moors are flushed purple, fields are in flower, the boggy bits are drier underfoot and the blue sky is flecked with little clouds, the Pennine Way seems perfect.

Spring and autumn can feature many fine days, and both seasons have their own particular charms. Spring sees the gradual greening of the landscape

Walking the Pennine Way in winter is reserved only for the most experienced long-distance walkers

Rain and mist on Cross Fell, where England's most extreme weather conditions have been recorded (Day 18)

and the first flowers of the year, while newborn lambs bleat plaintively in the lower pastures. Autumn sees the gradual ripening of seeds, hedgerow fruits at their best and cultivated crops ready for harvesting. The days, however, are notably shorter and there may well be cooler, wetter weather.

Winter can be severe in the Pennines, especially when rare falls of deep snow blanket the path and make route-finding particularly difficult. While winter traverses of the Pennine Way are rare, those walkers possessing the skills and stamina to complete the trek also have to cope with the fact that some facilities and services are absent. The hardiest walkers of all are those who aim to be self-sufficient and backpack the route in the winter months.

ACCOMMODATION

When the Pennine Way was opened, it was assumed that the bulk of walkers would carry full packs and camp at intervals along the trail. Many did, but there was also a good selection of youth hostels along the way, and the Youth Hostels Association once offered a service allowing walkers to book all their bed-nights in one fell swoop.

Things have changed over the years, and while many Wayfarers still camp, the availability of hostels has changed. Many walkers now choose to stay at bed and breakfasts (B&Bs), and some are quite happy to pay someone else to make all their arrangements for them, booking their long-distance walk through commercial trekking companies.

The Pennine Way has plenty of accommodation options, but they are

From the outset, it was imagined that walkers would camp every night along the Pennine Way. This pitch is at Tan Hill (Day 10)

unevenly spaced, and it is worth having details to hand as early as possible. The free 'Pennine Way Accommodation and Public Transport Guide' can be obtained from tourist information offices, or downloaded from www. nationaltrail.co.uk/pennineway. The Pennine Way Association also produces the 'Pennine Way Accommodation and Camping Guide', which can be downloaded from the association's website, www.penninewayassociation.co.uk.

FOOD AND DRINK

Most long-distance walkers start the day with a hearty breakfast, take a break along the way for lunch, and

like to have a good meal in the evenings. Those who like to walk in comfort can book themselves in places offering dinner, bed and breakfast, often with the option of a packed lunch for an additional charge. Youth hostels now offer full meals services and packed lunches.

Walkers who are backpacking need to know where all the useful shops are located so that they can buy more food as they travel, rather than carry everything for the duration of their trek. Towns have a range of shops, but some villages have either a limited choice or nothing at all. Be sure to read ahead to discover where resupply options are sparse, then buy

For those with a sweet tooth – the Dalesman Café and Sweet Emporium at Gargrave (Day 5)

Always be aware of opportunities to buy food and drink, especially where shops lie off-route (Day 4)

food in advance to cover for those days. Many Wayfarers like to take a break at a pub, and there are several along the Pennine Way, but unevenly spread and rarely in the middle of a day's walk. Places offering refreshment are duly noted in this guidebook. The most famous pub is surely the Tan Hill Inn, a convivial establishment in the middle of nowhere and the highest pub in England.

MONEY MATTERS

While an increasing number of shops, pubs and restaurants will accept payment by credit card, many don't, so walkers need to carry plenty of cash to pay for goods and services while on the move, especially on the more remote parts of the Pennine Way. If you are unsure about carrying large amounts of cash, at least try and budget ahead, then be aware of places along the way that have banks and ATMs – these are mentioned in the daily route descriptions and some small supermarkets offer a 'cashback' service.

COMMUNICATIONS

Mobile phones don't always get a signal along the Pennine Way, and coverage varies depending on your service provider. All of the towns and most of the villages along the Pennine Way have telephone kiosks, but rural kiosks are gradually being removed. For internet

31

access, wifi hotspots are exceedingly scarce and the best you could hope for is to be granted access by one of your accommodation providers. Post offices are noted where they exist.

PLANNING YOUR SCHEDULE

The Pennine Way is the toughest of the National Trails, so it suits those with previous long-distance walking experience. If you have no such experience then you should consider

gaining some before you go. Try a weekend walk here and there, staying overnight on your route. Progress to a week-long walk, preferably in upland terrain, carrying everything you would expect to carry on a long trek. Keep a check on your progress day by day and hour by hour, so that you know how long it takes you to cover varying distances and awkward terrain.

While some people have run the Pennine Way in as little as three days, most take two or three weeks to

Pennine Wayfarers must take the weather as it comes, but always check the forecast (Day 2)

walk the distance, and on average it tends to work out at around 18 days. As with all long-distance walks, take each day at a pace that is neither slow nor stressful, and the trek can be completed comfortably and enjoyably. Fatigue and foul weather can result in alterations to carefully planned schedules, so wise walkers will build a day or two into their plans to cover for such eventualities.

WHAT TO PACK

This depends primarily on your choice of accommodation. From its earliest days, the Pennine Way was intended to be a tough route for tough walkers. In the beginning, many walkers carried heavy packs and planned to camp every night. If camping, then full backpacking kit is required but keep everything as light as possible, taking advantage of modern materials and innovative products. There is no need for a full backpack to exceed ten kilos, and seldom any need to pack more than two days' worth of food.

Youth hostels were originally spartan, but gradually came to offer more comforts and a number of B&Bs sprang up along the route and these tend to be well supported by today's Pennine Wayfarers. Anyone using hostels or B&Bs needs little more than the usual contents of their daysack, plus a lightweight change of clothing for the evenings, allowing the 'walking' clothes to be rinsed and dried every couple of days or so. It really isn't necessary to carry heavy loads along the Pennine Way.

The Pennine Way is well signposted and is marked with a National Trail acorn logo throughout

WAYMARKING AND ACCESS

The Pennine Way is a designated right of way from start to finish, therefore it should be open at all times and free of obstructions. The route is made up of public footpaths, public bridleways, public byways and public highways. Signposts usually include the words 'Pennine Way', along with the official National Trail symbol of an acorn. Marker posts generally feature only the acorn symbol and a directional arrow. Occasionally, the initials 'PW' may be painted or carved onto surfaces to give additional directions.

Note that there are some very long stretches that have no signposts or markers, and this is the policy for what is after all a tough and often remote long-distance trail. In clear weather, providing careful note is taken of route directions, rudimentary map-reading skills will be enough. However, on some moorlands, especially in mist, an ability to use a map and a compass is a distinct advantage.

MAPS OF THE ROUTE

The Ordnance Survey covers the Pennine Way on 10 Landranger maps at a scale of 1:50,000. The sheet numbers are 74, 80, 86, 87, 91, 92, 98, 103, 109 and 110. Linear extracts from these maps are reproduced throughout this guidebook, with the route highlighted. For greater detail, eight Explorer maps cover the route at a scale of 1:25,000, and the sheet numbers are OL1, OL2, OL16, OL21, OL30, OL31, OL42 and OL43. Any or all of these maps can be ordered from the Ordnance Survey (www.ordnancesurvey.co.uk).

Harvey publishes three maps covering the Pennine Way on water-resistant paper at a scale of 1:40,000. These are Pennine Way South, Pennine Way Central and Pennine Way North (www.harveymaps.co.uk). The relevant maps for each stage of the Pennine Way are listed at the start of each day's walk.

EMERGENCIES

The Pennines and Cheviot Hills are not particularly dangerous, and the biggest problem unwary walkers are likely to face is the prospect of losing their way on a featureless moorland. However, accidents and injuries could occur almost anywhere on the route and the intervention of the emergency services might be required. To contact the police, ambulance, fire service or mountain rescue, use a telephone to call 999 (or the European emergency number 112), and state clearly the nature of the emergency. Give them your telephone number and, most importantly, keep in touch while a response is mounted.

DAY 1

Edale to Crowden

Start	Railway Station, Edale, SK 123 853
Finish	Youth Hostel, Crowden, SK 073 993
Distance	29km (18 miles)
Ascent	740m (2430ft)
Descent	780m (2560ft)
Maps	OS Landranger 110, OS Explorer OL1, Harvey's Pennine Way South
Terrain	Broad, high and exposed boggy moorlands, with several stretches of firm flagstone path. However, careful navigation is required in mist.
Refreshments	None between Edale and Crowden, and very limited at Crowden.

The Pennine Way originally left Edale in two directions. The 'main' route made a direct ascent of Kinder Scout, crossing soft peat bogs that proved very confusing in mist, while the 'alternative' route skirted round the edge of the plateau. The top of Kinder Scout got badly over-trodden, so the Pennine Way now follows only one route out of Edale, staying on firm ground. The moors between Kinder Scout and Bleaklow were once trodden into a filthy quagmire, but now boast fine, firm paths. However, bear in mind that this is a hard day's walk, and some walkers realise only too late that they are not equal to the task!

Map continued
on page 38

35

EDALE

This little village can be overwhelmed by visitors, especially on summer weekends. If arriving by train, simply follow the road a short way into the village. The Moorland Centre is worth visiting, packed with information about the Peak District National Park and local services. It is open daily throughout the year (free entry, tel: 01433 670207). There are a couple of pubs and cafés, as well as a post office and general store, which also has an ATM. If you are planning to stay overnight, there are campsites, a youth hostel nearby and B&Bs.

The Pennine Way starts in the centre of **Edale** at The Old Nags Head. The first signpost is across the road from the pub, pointing to a well-trodden path climbing gently beside a little streambed flanked by trees. Emerge and turn left to follow a flagstone path up through a few fields, with fine views back through the dale. Continue gently up an earth path through a couple more fields, then head downhill through more fields to pick up an enclosed path and track past **Upper Booth Farm**, which has a campsite and camping barn.

Turn right along a narrow road, crossing a bridge over a stream, then pass fields to reach **Lee Farm**. The Lee Barn Information Shelter is here, containing interesting notices and offering shelter from inclement weather, courtesy of the National Trust. Follow a track onwards, passing through gates from field to field to reach a narrow, stone packhorse bridge at the foot of **Jacob's Ladder**.

Turn left or right – left being a long and stony loop once used by packhorses, right being a shorter, steeper, stone-pitched path. Both routes meet at a cairn and a stony path climbs onwards. Towards the top a short-cut to the right has recently been paved with flagstones. Either turn right along the flagstone path, or climb to a gate, then turn right. Both routes join and climb a short, steep slope of grass, with tufts of bilberry. When a sprawling cairn is reached in a slight dip, keep left to follow a clear path, passing big boulders and gritstone outcrops. Take care in mist while crossing broad, bare peat covered with

The Pennine Way starts, whatever the weather, at the Old Nags Head in the village of Edale

Map continued
on page 40

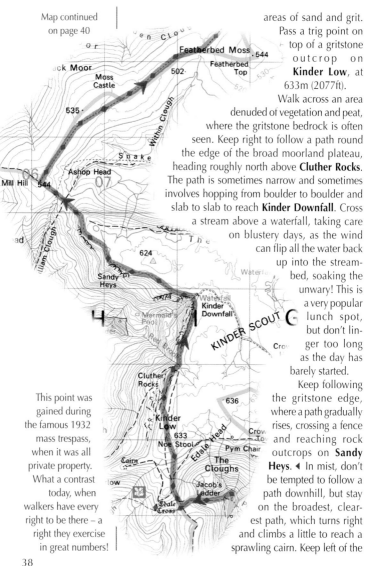

areas of sand and grit.
Pass a trig point on
top of a gritstone
outcrop on
Kinder Low, at
633m (2077ft).

Walk across an area
denuded of vegetation and peat,
where the gritstone bedrock is often
seen. Keep right to follow a path round
the edge of the broad moorland plateau,
heading roughly north above **Cluther Rocks**.
The path is sometimes narrow and sometimes
involves hopping from boulder to boulder and
slab to slab to reach **Kinder Downfall**. Cross
a stream above a waterfall, taking care
on blustery days, as the wind
can flip all the water back
up into the stream-
bed, soaking the
unwary! This is
a very popular
lunch spot,
but don't lin-
ger too long
as the day has
barely started.

Keep following
the gritstone edge,
where a path gradually
rises, crossing a fence
and reaching rock
outcrops on **Sandy
Heys**. ◀ In mist, don't
be tempted to follow a
path downhill, but stay
on the broadest, clear-
est path, which turns right
and climbs a little to reach a
sprawling cairn. Keep left of the

This point was
gained during
the famous 1932
mass trespass,
when it was all
private property.
What a contrast
today, when
walkers have every
right to be there – a
right they exercise
in great numbers!

A fine flagstone path leaves Mill Hill with ease, looking back towards Kinder Scout

cairn to pick up a steep, stone-pitched path leading down to the grassy gap of **Ashop Head**, around 510m (1675ft).

A flagstone path heads left, but the Pennine Way keeps right along a broad and stony path. Pass a prominent marker post where another path crosses, and climb straight over a grassy hump to reach another gap. A flagstone path climbs straight uphill, giving way to a broad, stony path to a cairn at 544m (1785ft) on top of **Mill Hill**. Paths cross on the summit, so turn right to follow another flagstone path onwards.

This used to be one of the worst areas of bog on the Pennine Way, but the path now offers a firm, dry footing. The old path can often be seen on the left as a black, boggy line, though it is slowly re-vegetating. The moorland is predominantly grassy, with areas of bog cotton, sphagnum moss, rushes, bilberry and heather. ▶ The path undulates very gently and writhes to avoid awkward boggy areas on Moss Castle and **Featherbed Moss**. There is a strange sight ahead, where vehicles apparently speed straight across the moor since the surface of the A57 road on the **Snake Pass** isn't seen until it is reached at a gate. Cross the road with care, as the traffic is very fast.

Look out for cloudberries, a distinctive arctic remnant plant that positively thrives on the highest and bleakest boggy moorlands.

SNAKE PASS

There are no snakes hereabouts. Originally, there was a Snake Inn, whose sign bore a snake emblem that

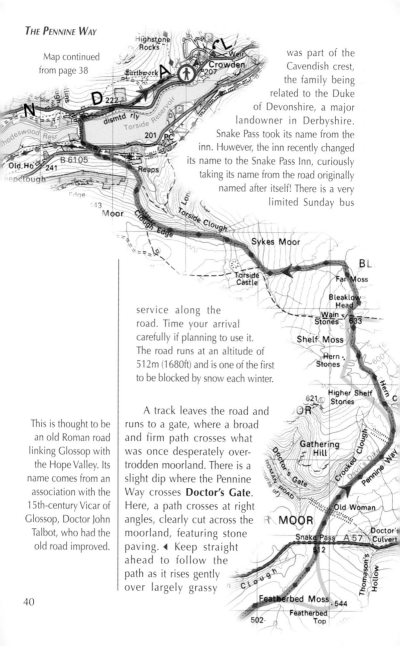

Map continued
from page 38

was part of the
Cavendish crest,
the family being
related to the Duke
of Devonshire, a major
landowner in Derbyshire.
Snake Pass took its name from the
inn. However, the inn recently changed
its name to the Snake Pass Inn, curiously
taking its name from the road originally
named after itself! There is a very
limited Sunday bus

service along the
road. Time your arrival
carefully if planning to use it.
The road runs at an altitude of
512m (1680ft) and is one of the first
to be blocked by snow each winter.

A track leaves the road and
runs to a gate, where a broad
and firm path crosses what
was once desperately over-
trodden moorland. There is a
slight dip where the Pennine
Way crosses **Doctor's Gate**.
Here, a path crosses at right
angles, clearly cut across the
moorland, featuring stone
paving. ◄ Keep straight
ahead to follow the
path as it rises gently
over largely grassy

This is thought to be
an old Roman road
linking Glossop with
the Hope Valley. Its
name comes from an
association with the
15th-century Vicar of
Glossop, Doctor John
Talbot, who had the
old road improved.

moorland, with heather and bilberry more noticeable while following a flagstone path. A few steps lead down into **Devil's Dike**, a deep cutting in the peat where the stony ground beneath has been exposed. In wet weather it can carry a stream. A gradual ascent through the cutting links with more flagstones, then the path becomes a stony channel flanked by peat. Another stretch of flagstones leads to **Hern Clough**.

Turn left to follow this upstream, crossing and re-crossing as necessary. Later, there are more flagstones, as well as a series of helpful marker stones bearing carved directional arrows. The broad and peaty top of **Bleaklow Head** is worn to sand and grit in places, with the summit cairn bearing a wooden stake at 633m (2077ft). Views south are blocked by the plateau of Kinder Scout. Other prominent features include distant Winter Hill and Pendle Hill, with Black Hill closer to hand. In very clear conditions, Pen-y-Ghent can be seen far ahead, maybe as much as a week away via the Pennine Way.

To leave Bleaklow Head, make a slight left turn, confirming the correct path by looking for 'PW' carved on a rock. A narrow and gentle path heads roughly north-west down a slope dominated by bilberry. The path becomes rather awkward, with stones and boulders underfoot on the way down a heathery slope. There are some stretches

A firm flagstone path crosses what was once badly over-trodden moorland on the way to Bleaklow

of flagstones, but the path is quite rugged as it leads down to a confluence of streams. Ford both streams then climb up a short, steep slope above **Torside Clough**.

The Pennine Way runs along a heathery edge, passing a few gritstone outcrops overlooking the stream. It can be rugged as it runs downhill, but a good stretch on flagstones crosses a fence. At a junction of paths, keep right downhill, later climbing to traverse **Clough Edge**. There is a view down to Torside Reservoir, with Black Hill beyond. A stone-pitched path descends steeply from the edge, passing through a gate in a fence. Turn left down a broader path, keeping left of the farmhouse at **Reaps**, following its access track to the **B6105 road**. Turn left here if staying nearby at The Old House B&B, otherwise cross the road as signposted for the Pennine Way.

Turn right to reach some cobbles then turn sharp left down a short tarmac road. This gives way to a track across the dam of **Torside Reservoir**, overlooking Rhodeswood Reservoir. Climb stone steps from the reservoir dam and cross a track to spot a Pennine Way signpost. Turn right to follow a path through a belt of pine trees between Torside Reservoir and a busy road. After passing through a gate, turn left up log steps. Cross the busy **A628 road** and turn right through a gate. A narrow tarmac road runs gently uphill through gates. When it runs downhill through a gate, the Pennine Way is signposted off to the left, for those who wish to continue. Otherwise, keep walking straight down the road and cross a river to reach **Crowden**.

CROWDEN

Facilties are extremely limited in the village – there is only a campsite and a youth hostel. The hostel operates as an outdoor education centre and if it is occupied by schoolchildren, you cannot stay. Check in advance, and if necessary, break your journey early at The Old House, which offers B&B and bunkrooms. Food supplies at Crowden are limited to whatever the campsite and hostel stock. The main road has a bus service linking Sheffield and Liverpool.

DAY 2

Crowden to Standedge

Start	Youth Hostel, Crowden, SK 073 993
Finish	A62 road, Standedge, SE 018 095
Distance	20km (12½ miles)
Ascent	660m (2165ft)
Descent	480m (1575ft)
Maps	OS Landranger 110, OS Explorer OL1, Harvey's Pennine Way South
Terrain	Mostly moorland walking, with several stretches paved with flagstones, but a couple of wet and boggy areas remain. One stretch uses a firm path through a valley, passing reservoirs.
Refreshments	Snoopy's snack van *might* be parked at Wessenden Head. Pubs off-route at Standedge.

Black Hill once had a fearsome reputation among Pennine Wayfarers, with its broad top covered in deep black bogs. The hill now bears a long line of firm flagstones. The 'black' has gone, replaced by 'green' as the whole top has been re-vegetated. The Pennine Way 'main' route originally headed directly to Standedge across appalling bogs, with an 'alternative' seeking firm ground via Wessenden. These days, there is only one designated route, which runs via Wessenden. Standedge is completely lacking facilities, so walkers will need to detour off-route to find food, drink and lodgings.

If starting from **Crowden**, retrace your steps back up the narrow road from the river and turn right as signposted for the Pennine Way. There are short-cuts from the hostel, for those who don't mind missing a stretch of the route. The path rises through gates to reach a small plantation on the hillside. Beyond are slopes of bracken, where the path becomes awkward due to stones protruding from the ground. Heather and bilberry are apparent as the path passes below **Black Tor**, where a quarried edge bears patchy woodland. The path undulates and crosses

43

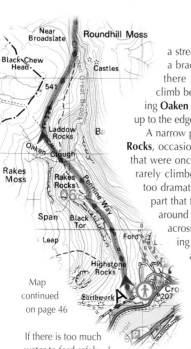

a stream, then climbs, steep and rugged, up a bracken slope. When the path levels out, there are fine views along the valley. The climb becomes steep and rugged again, crossing **Oaken Clough** to pick up a stone-pitched path up to the edge of a heather moorland.

A narrow path wanders along the top of **Laddow Rocks**, occasionally offering views of gritstone crags that were once popular with rock climbers, but are rarely climbed these days. The crag doesn't look too dramatic, but keep looking back to spot one part that features an overhang. The path rises to around 500m (1640ft), then descends gradually across a slope of grass and bilberry, becoming boggy and over-trodden as it runs parallel to **Crowden Great Brook**.

Step across a tributary and walk parallel to the main stream on a firm path. Cross another tributary, then when the main stream bites into a shale bank, cross and re-cross the flow to continue. ◄ The path gets wet and boggy and walkers often detour too far from the stream, thereby missing the start of a firm, dry flagstone path. This pulls away from the stream, leading to a stile over a fence on **Grains Moss**.

Map continued on page 46

If there is too much water to ford safely, simply climb over the top of the shale bank and pick up the path later.

Simply follow the flagstone path straight up a grassy, rushy slope polka-dotted with bog cotton. Cross a boggy rise at **Dun Hill**, then the flagstones end for a while. A firm path passes peat hags that are being stabilised against erosion. Another length of flagstones lead over the broad moorland summit of **Black Hill**, passing through a pool of water at one point, reaching a trig point with a paved 'patio' of flagstones around it at 582m (1908ft).

BLACK HILL

The summit of Black Hill was for many years trodden to death, leaving not even a blade of grass. The bog was so over-trodden that it was often impossible to reach

Laddow Rocks were once popular with rock climbers, but are seldom climbed today

the trig point, which stood on a firm 'island' known as Soldier's Lump. The name derived from a time when Ordnance Survey 'sappers' set up camp on the hill while surveying the land. The trig point they planted on the summit was close to collapse after the wholesale erosion of peat in recent years, but it has been stoutly buttressed. The 'Moors for the Future' project (**www.moorsforthefuture.org.uk**) has successfully re-vegetated the summit of Black Hill with grass, bog cotton and bilberry. The Pennine Way has been confined to a single firm, dry, erosion-proof line across the moors.

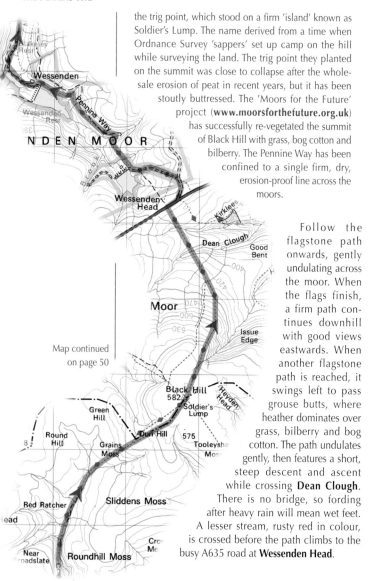

Map continued on page 50

Follow the flagstone path onwards, gently undulating across the moor. When the flags finish, a firm path continues downhill with good views eastwards. When another flagstone path is reached, it swings left to pass grouse butts, where heather dominates over grass, bilberry and bog cotton. The path undulates gently, then features a short, steep descent and ascent while crossing **Dean Clough**. There is no bridge, so fording after heavy rain will mean wet feet. A lesser stream, rusty red in colour, is crossed before the path climbs to the busy A635 road at **Wessenden Head**.

Turn right to follow the road with care. If Snoopy's snack van is parked here, then by all means take a break for food and drink, otherwise turn left up the minor road signposted for Meltham and Huddersfield. Turn left down through a gate to follow a track straight down to **Wessenden Head Reservoir**. There is a fine view down the valley to another reservoir, and a house among trees, with the distinctive profile of Pule Hill beyond. ▸

The land from here to White Hill (Day 3) makes up the extensive National Trust Marsden Moor Estate.

Walk straight down a broad and clear path. This makes a couple of loops round little side valleys to reach the dam of **Wessenden Reservoir**. Follow a track downhill from the dam, catching a glimpse of **Wessenden Lodge** behind tall deer fences. The track rises gently to reach a signpost. At this point, turn left for the Pennine Way, down a path on a steep slope of bracken. If planning to visit Marsden, however, keep straight along the track and see the later route description.

WESSENDEN RESERVOIRS

The Wessenden Reservoirs are piled one on top of another in a narrow valley. Construction was financed by a consortium of mill owners in Marsden, whose mills were located beside the River Colne. The reservoirs were completed in 1800, shortly after the opening of the Huddersfield Narrow Canal. The mill owners jealously guarded their water supply and weren't keen for any of it to be used to be used by the canal company.

Cross a footbridge and climb steeply up a rugged path on a slope of heather. The gradient eases at a stone-built structure, where there is a view down the valley to Blakeley Reservoir. The path is almost level as it reaches a stream. Cross over and climb up stone steps, then continue along a flagstone path through bracken. A length of stony path is followed by more flagstones, and **Black Moss** is surely misnamed when masses of white bog cotton nod in the breeze. Pule Hill is seen across Swellands Reservoir, while the Pennine Way crosses a dam on **Black Moss Reservoir**, where there are a couple of sandy beaches.

BLACK MOSS AND SWELLANDS RESERVOIRS

These two reservoirs, along with four others, were constructed on the high moors to supply the Huddersfield Narrow Canal. A system of drains catches little streams and feeds the water into the reservoirs. Black Moss Reservoir has a dam at either end, being constructed on a broad moorland gap. The dam of Swellands Reservoir broke in November 1810, sending a deluge of peaty water down to Marsden, where it caused great damage in what was called 'The Night of the Black Flood'.

Overshoot the end of the dam before turning left. The path follows a fence to a corner. Keep straight ahead before turning right up a flagstone path, going through a gate in a fence from grassy moorland to heather moorland. Walk downhill and go through another gate, back onto grassy moorland. The flagstones end at a small stream, where a left turn leads up a track on a stout embankment overlooking **Redbrook Reservoir**, another feeder for the Huddersfield Narrow Canal. The track leads up through a gate, crossing a crest parallel to the busy **A62 road**, which runs through a deep cutting. Descend to the roadside beside Brunclough Reservoir at **Standedge**, at 387m (1270ft). The Peak District National Park ends beside the main road.

STANDEDGE

There are no facilities where the Pennine Way crosses the road at Standedge, so extra distance must be covered in search of accommodation, food and drink. Following the main road is not recommended, as it is too busy. Walkers heading for one of the two nearby pubs – the Great Western and the Carriage House – should note that these were the buildings seen closest to Redbrook Reservoir. A direct approach from the Pennine Way is possible, though the ground is boggy underfoot. Anyone heading further off-route can either catch a bus, or if they insist on walking, can use the following routes to reach Marsden or Diggle.

Off-route to Diggle

Diggle lies 2.5km (1½ miles) off-route, with a descent of 180m (590ft). To reach it, don't cross the main road at **Standedge**, but walk between the road and **Brunclough Reservoir**. Walk down from the reservoir to a clear track to find a Pennine Bridleway signpost. Turn left down a track marked for Diggle, passing a derelict house. Turn right at a marker post and stay on the clearest path downhill, passing a spoil heap and reaching a house on the hillside. Continue down a walled and fenced track past fields, reaching a tarmac road at the Diggle Hotel. Turn right at a road junction to cross a railway then turn left to walk into **Diggle**.

A Pennine Wayfarer forges through heather above Redbrook Reservoir near Standedge

DIGGLE

The village has two pubs, a shop and a couple of places offering accommodation. Buses run through the village, linking Manchester, Standedge and Huddersfield. The entrances to the railway and canal tunnels can be seen fairly close together.

Walkers heading off-route to Marsden can reach the town by descending a flight of 211 stone steps

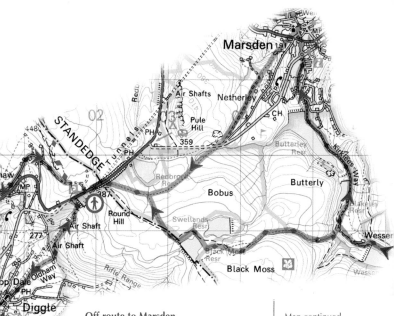

Off-route to Marsden

Map continued from page 46

Marsden lies 3km (2 miles) off-route, with a descent of 140m (460ft). After passing **Wessenden Lodge**, simply follow the clear track down through the valley. Pass **Blakeley Reservoir** and follow the track onwards past **Butterley Reservoir**. Turn left when a road is reached, and while this could be followed into town, turn left down a flight of 211 stone steps instead. Turn right to follow a track through a wood before passing between tall mills on the outskirts of **Marsden**. Turn left down a road and pass a small roundabout. Follow Fall Lane and fork left to pass through a tunnel. Turn right along Towngate to follow a river into the town centre.

MARSDEN

Pennine Wayfarers started visiting Marsden many years ago when it had a youth hostel, but there are other accommodation options. The town has a post office, shops, pubs, cafés and a tourist information centre (tel: 01484 845595). Regular daily buses link Marsden with

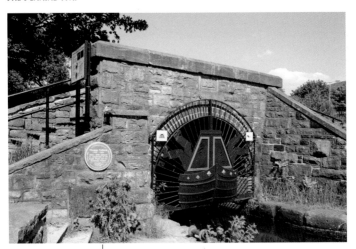

Entrance to the Huddersfield Canal tunnel at Diggle, cut beneath Standedge between 1794 and 1811

Huddersfield, Standedge and Manchester. Regular daily trains link Marsden with Manchester and Huddersfield. To learn more about the various tunnels under Standedge, take a stroll to the Standedge Tunnel Visitor Centre.

STANDEDGE TUNNELS

There are actually four tunnels under Standedge, all measuring a little over 5km (3 miles) in length. A narrow canal tunnel was constructed first, between 1794 and 1811. It was the highest canal in Britain at 147m (645ft) above sea level, but also the deepest underground, lying 145m (638ft) below Standedge. A single-track rail tunnel was cut between 1846 and 1849, followed by another one between 1868 and 1870. A twin-track rail tunnel was built last, between 1890 and 1894. Dozens of transverse tunnels link all four tunnels together, primarily between the rail tunnels and the canal tunnel, for the purpose of extracting waste. The Standedge Tunnel Visitor Centre is only a stroll from Marsden, open throughout the year except Mondays (free entry, tel: 01484 844298, **www.standedge.co.uk**).

The detour to Marsden leaves Pennine Wayfarers in a quandary. Do they walk back to Wessenden to pick up the route to Standedge? Catch a bus? Short-cut to Standedge? The following route is a direct short-cut, measuring 3km (2 miles) back to the Pennine Way, with an ascent of 150m (490ft).

Leave **Marsden** by walking along Towngate, climbing beside the churchyard to reach the main **A62 road**. Cross the road and climb a short way up Old Mount Road. Turn right as signposted 'public footpath' and follow a track towards an isolated house. Turn left beforehand as indicated by a marker post. The way is overgrown for a bit until a stile is crossed. A deep-cut, rushy groove climbs up a grassy slope, with fine views of Marsden and its mills. Keep to the left of the groove to follow a track up to a farmhouse.

Go through gates to pass the farmhouse and climb straight up another grassy slope. Pick up and follow another path in a groove, passing through a gate and climbing to join a broad, clear, stony track. Follow this straight ahead, gently uphill, with fine views back to Marsden, as well as to Black Hill and the moors above Wessenden. The track levels out and rejoins Old Mount Road, which itself drops down to another road.

Cross the road to reach a public footpath sign, and drop down a little to cross a stream. Climb a little and keep right, watching for a grassy path and a marker post. Simply walk straight ahead, gently up the moorland slope, always following the grassy path. After crossing a crest, **Redbrook Reservoir** comes into view. The path runs along an embankment, and there is a prominent notch where a stream crosses. Beyond this is a clear track, which is the Pennine Way, leading directly to **Standedge** at 387m (1270ft).

DAY 3
Standedge to Callis Bridge

Start	A62 road, Standedge, SE 018 095
Finish	Callis Bridge, Hebden Bridge, SD 972 264
Distance	26km (16 miles)
Ascent	350m (1150ft)
Descent	640m (2100ft)
Maps	OS Landranger 103, 109 and 110, OS Explorer OL1 and OL 21, Harvey's Pennine Way South
Terrain	Gentle moorland walking on good paths gives way to rugged paths on Blackstone Edge. Broad, firm, level reservoir tracks allow speedy progress. Moorland paths and farm tracks later.
Refreshments	Snack van at Bleakedgate. The White House pub. Plenty of choice off-route at Hebden Bridge.

This is a relatively easy stretch of the Pennine Way. Low, gently rolling moorlands give way to the rough and rocky crest of Blackstone Edge. A series of firm, level tracks follow reservoir drains, where it is possible to stride out with confidence and pick up speed. The stout, stone monument of Stoodley Pike is seen from time to time. Walkers agree that no matter how much distance is covered, it never seems to draw nearer! At the end of the day there is a descent into post-industrial Calderdale, where the bustling little town of Hebden Bridge can be reached by a short detour off-route.

Anyone following the Pennine Bridleway will find two B&Bs within easy reach. The first is Rock Farm, situated below the gritstone outcrop of Standedge, and the second is Wellcroft House, located at a crossroads at Bleak Hey Nook.

Start where Pennine Way crosses the busy A62 road on **Standedge**, following a clear track uphill. Keep straight ahead at a junction, and keep straight ahead when the Pennine Way and Pennine Bridleway run concurrent for a short distance. At the top of this track, the Pennine Way turns right, crossing a stile over a fence, while the Pennine Bridleway continues straight ahead. ◄

A well-worn path leads away from the track, up a grassy slope. Cross a stile and follow the line of a fence, then cross another stile and climb uphill as a low, rocky edge develops along **Standedge**. A trig point is passed at 448m (1470ft). The path continues gently, becoming broad and stony, with a low rocky edge to the left and denuded peat to the right. A dip is reached where a stone marks the Oldham Way down to the left and the Pennine Way up to the right. A firm gravel path undulates over tussocky moorland with bog cotton and rushes. A footbridge is crossed just before the **A640 road** is reached at a small car park.

Cross the road and pick up a path just to the left, climbing up the grassy, rushy slopes of **Denshaw Moor**. Follow a tumbled wall and a fence over a moorland crest with a pool on top. Bog cotton is abundant on the moors. Walk downhill and cross a stream, with a brief glimpse left down to Readycon Dean Reservoir. Walk uphill and cross a fence to leave the extensive National Trust Marsden Moor Estate. The grassy top of **White Hill** bears a trig point at 466m (1529ft), with a view of Rochdale below the moors. The path swings right along a high crest and descends gently to the A672 road on **Bleakedgate Moor**, where a snack van may be parked.

Cross the road and follow a path over a grassy moor. Cross the access road serving a prominent communication mast on **Windy Hill**. The path drops downhill and is covered in flagstones as it approaches the exceptionally busy **M62 motorway**. ▶ Once across, turn left up a stony path, pass through a gate, then head gently downhill on a grassy, rushy moor. Cross a boggy little stream and climb

Map continued
on page 58

The M62 was opened in 1971, six years after the Pennine Way. A footbridge was installed for Pennine Wayfarers, who look down on the endless flow of traffic and wonder 'What's the rush?'

55

The gritstone outcrop on Blackstone Edge is low, but views are remarkably extensive

gently uphill across slopes of bog cotton, with Green Withens Reservoir seen down to the right. There are areas of bare peat and lots of exposed gritstone boulders towards the top of **Blackstone Edge**. Pass a trig point perched on a rocky outcrop at 472m (1549ft). Although the gritstone edge is low, it is remarkably rugged and attractive, and views stretch from the wild moors to urban lowlands, taking in the West Pennines, Whittle Hill, Pendle Hill, Black Hameldon, Boulsworth Hill and Stoodley Pike.

BLACKSTONE EDGE

This hill, more than any other on the Pennine Way, seems to have excited the imaginations of past travellers. Celia Fiennes crossed it in 1698 and wrote: 'Then I Came to Blackstone Edge noted all over England for a dismal high precipice... very troublesome as its a moist ground soe as is usual on these high hills; they stagnate the aire and hold mist and raines almost perpetually... This hill took me up Much tyme to gaine the top and alsoe to descend it and put me in mind of the Description of ye Alpes in Italy.'

Daniel Defoe crossed Blackstone Edge in 1724, in a blizzard in August! He wrote: 'the narrowness

The Aiggin Stone is a medieval moorland marker high on the 'Roman road' on Blackstone Edge

of the way, look'd horrible to us...we knew nothing where we were, or whether we were right or wrong... the main hill which we came down from...is properly called Blackstone Edge, or, by the country people, the Edge...' Elsewhere in the same letter he described it as 'the Andes of England'.

The path descends at a slight gradient, but is rugged and stony, winding between boulders. It rises a little and crosses a stile over a fence to reach the medieval moorland marker of the **Aiggin Stone**. Turn left downhill to follow an old, grooved track down the moorland slope. This becomes a splendid paved track, often referred to as a 'Roman road'. The small town of Littleborough is seen far below.

THE 'ROMAN ROAD'

While it is likely that the Romans crossed the Pennines near Blackstone Edge, it is certain that they were not responsible for the fine stone paving on the route. The splendid causeway, with its two cobbled lanes and central gutter, was probably constructed after the passing of the first Blackstone Edge Turnpike Act of 1734. A

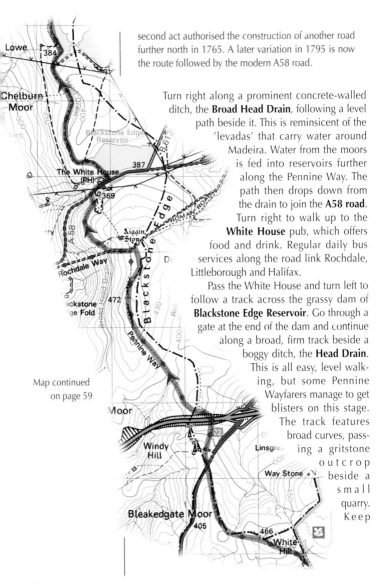

second act authorised the construction of another road further north in 1765. A later variation in 1795 is now the route followed by the modern A58 road.

Turn right along a prominent concrete-walled ditch, the **Broad Head Drain**, following a level path beside it. This is reminiscent of the 'levadas' that carry water around Madeira. Water from the moors is fed into reservoirs further along the Pennine Way. The path then drops down from the drain to join the **A58 road**. Turn right to walk up to the **White House** pub, which offers food and drink. Regular daily bus services along the road link Rochdale, Littleborough and Halifax.

Pass the White House and turn left to follow a track across the grassy dam of **Blackstone Edge Reservoir**. Go through a gate at the end of the dam and continue along a broad, firm track beside a boggy ditch, the **Head Drain**. This is all easy, level walking, but some Pennine Wayfarers manage to get blisters on this stage. The track features broad curves, passing a gritstone outcrop beside a small quarry. Keep

Map continued on page 59

58

straight ahead at track junctions to pass beneath a prominent pylon line on **Chelburn Moor**.

The track runs along the dam of **Light Hazzles Reservoir**. This is a rather forlorn, narrow and shallow reservoir that never holds enough water to reach its own draw-off tower, which is marooned on dry land. Further along, you will see that the dam was lowered. The track continues along the dam of **Warland Reservoir**. Around the middle of this long dam a draw-off tower is passed. At the end of the dam, the track follows the prominent stone-built **Warland Drain**, turning right at a

Map continued on page 61

settling tank. The track gives way to a path as the drain is followed upstream across **Langfield Common**. When the drain turns sharp right, turn left instead, as signposted for the Pennine Way.

THE RESERVOIRS

Blackstone Edge Reservoir, Chelburn Reservoir, Light Hazzles Reservoir and Warland Reservoir were constructed to feed the Rochdale Canal far below. In *A Treatise on Canals and Reservoirs*, published in 1816, John Sutcliffe wrote: 'The reservoirs will be filled twice in the year, and will give 8,871,720 tons of water in that period. If 8,871,720 be divided by 84,000, the amount of supposed tonnage, the product will be nearly 106 tons of water for every ton of goods supposed to be navigated on the line in one year.'

A flagstone path leads across a grassy, rushy moorland with areas of bog cotton. Pass a couple of prominent old boundary stones and follow a firm trodden path past gritstone boulders. Looking down to the right, Withens Clough Reservoir can be seen. When a dip in the moorland edge is reached, there are views along Calderdale, with Pendle Hill seen beyond. The little mill town of Todmorden is seen, with the village of Mankinholes closer to hand, while Stoodley Pike lies ahead. Follow the well-trodden path across the dip and up to a well-marked junction with an old paved 'causey'. The Pennine Way climbs straight ahead, but some walkers detour down to **Mankinholes**.

MANKINHOLES

This little village is easily reached by walking down an old paved 'causey', linking with the course of the Pennine Bridleway. Mankinholes is 1km (½ mile) off-route, with a descent of 150m (490ft). Facilities include a youth hostel and a farmhouse B&B with campsite, and there is a pub in the adjacent village of Lumbutts.

Staying on the Pennine Way, the path climbs past a prominent upright stone, then rises more gently and winds along a boulder-strewn edge. It is dry and firm underfoot and runs almost level as it reaches **Stoodley Pike**.

STOODLEY PIKE

This rather dark and grim monument, splattered with graffiti, was built following the exile of Napoleon to Elba in 1814. When he escaped, building work ceased. After the Battle of Waterloo in 1815 work recommenced and the monument was completed. In 1855 the whole thing collapsed and it was rebuilt in 1856. Spiral steps lead up to a parapet for more wide-ranging views. The monument is a landmark throughout this part of the South Pennines.

Map continued from page 59

Follow the path onwards down a grassy slope, away from the monument, to reach a junction of drystone

The monument on Stoodley Pike is a landmark throughout Calderdale and the South Pennines

walls. Go through a gap stile and continue ahead, then turn left over a stone step-stile. A path leads across and down a grassy, rushy moorland slope, reaching a track carrying the Pennine Bridleway. Cross over the track to follow the Pennine Way alongside a wall. Cross a stile filling an old stone gateway and follow the wall until it turns right. Cross a stile on the right and head diagonally across a rushy field. Go through a gate at the corner of a wall then follow the wall straight to a farm at **Lower Rough Head**.

The farm stands on a corner of a track, and the track runs gently downhill, flanked by walls, passing big fields. Go through a gate and walk down through a wood. This is predominantly oak and birch, but contains other trees. Keep to the main track as it heads downhill, except when a house comes into view, where a path short-cuts a bend on a slope of birch. The track continues down into the valley, crossing the Rochdale Canal and **River Calder** to reach the busy A646 road at **Callis Bridge**.

HEBDEN BRIDGE

Callis Bridge has nothing but regular daily buses to and from Hebden Bridge, linking with Halifax and Burnley. A detour into Hebden Bridge is easily made along the Rochdale Canal towpath for 1.5km (1 mile). Attractive houseboats, bridges, locks, a canal-side pub and Alternative Technology Centre are seen on the way to the town centre. Facilties include banks with ATMs, a post office, shops, pubs, cafés and restaurants. Regular daily buses run to Halifax and Burnley. There are daily buses to Blackshaw Head, with summer weekend buses to Widdop, further along the Pennine Way. Regular daily trains run to Halifax, York, Burnley and Preston. The Hebden Bridge Visitor and Canal Centre incorporates a tourist information centre (tel: 01422 843831).

DAY 4
Callis Bridge to Ickornshaw

Start	Callis Bridge, Hebden Bridge, SD 972 264
Finish	Ickornshaw, Cowling, SD 965 428
Distance	26km (16 miles)
Ascent	880m (2885ft)
Descent	760m (2490ft)
Maps	OS Landranger 103, OS Explorer OL21, Harvey's Pennine Way South
Terrain	Fiddly paths and tracks need to be linked to climb towards the moors. There are several ascents and descents during the day. Most moorland paths are firm and most boggy stretches have been surfaced with flagstones.
Refreshments	Pubs or cafés off-route at Jack Bridge, Colden, Blake Dean, Ponden and Cowling.

Throughout the climb from Calderdale, maps and route descriptions need to be read carefully, and watch for signposts and waymarks. The area has an incredibly dense network of rights of way, and it is easy to be drawn off course. During the day, there are virtually no facilities actually on the Pennine Way, but there are a number of pubs, cafés and even a shop lying very close to the route. The higher moors are quite easily crossed and the fringes of 'Brontë Country' are visited. Some walkers break this day's walk at Ponden, or head off-route to Haworth, either on foot or by bus.

Use the pedestrian crossing on the busy A646 road at **Callis Bridge**. The Pennine Bridleway turns left and the Pennine Way turns right. They run roughly parallel for half a day until they meet again. The Pennine Way quickly leaves the main road by turning left up Underbank Avenue, going under the stone arch of a railway bridge to reach Lacy Houses.

Climb straight up a steep, cobbled path flanked by walls and, in summer, foxgloves. Swing left to join a track past a few houses, and a narrow road runs up to a ruined

Map continued
on page 69

chapel and an overgrown graveyard. Turn right here, where a sign offers a choice of 'Official Route' or 'Wainwright Route', which are at odds with each other for a while. The official route crosses a stile beside a gate and follows a well-vegetated path making a rising traverse across a slope. There are good views of Calderdale, with Stoodley Pike beyond. A steeper climb features stone steps, passing a curious little building spanning a rusty-coloured stream. Climb past this, and a house, to reach a track.

Turn left up the track, which becomes a narrow road rising gently past a house at Long Hey. Turn right as signposted through a gap in a wall, following a path straight up through fields. Keep right of one farm and left of

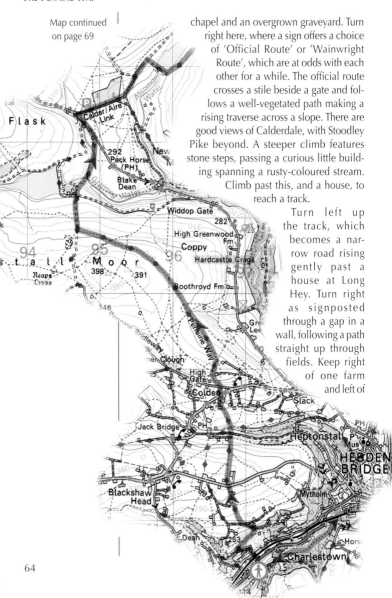

another, walking up a track to a road near **Blackshaw Head**. Cross the road and climb through a field to the left of **Badger Fields Farm**, where there is accommodation.

Walk down through fields. The path becomes rather awkward underfoot where it is constricted between narrow stone walls. A track on the left can be used to reach the New Delight Inn, lodgings and camping at **Jack Bridge**, otherwise walk further down the narrow path and cross another track. Stone steps lead down to **Colden Water**.

Cross the river using a stout 'clapper' bridge made of four long stone blocks. Climb stone steps at a gentle gradient, but watch for a left turn up a steeper flight of steps. Continue up through fields towards houses at **Colden**, but turn left as marked towards another house. Follow its cobbled access road up to a road close to a bus shelter. Buses run daily between here and Hebden Bridge. Cross the road and walk up a path to reach another road. There is a view back to Stoodley Pike, as well as a sign inviting a detour to the left. ▶

The road leads to a remarkable little shop at High Gate, describing itself as an 'Aladdin's Cave'. This is surprisingly busy with local folk, and offers food, drink and camping.

Walking high on Heptonstall Moor between Colden and Gorple, with Heptonstall seen in the distance

If the shop isn't required, pick up the Pennine Way across the road and climb up a narrow path in a deep groove, reaching a little gate. Swing left up through fields and go through another little gate onto heather moorland. Follow a wall over a crest until level with a farm. Turn left as signposted, walking gradually down a path across the moor. When a wall is reached, do not cross it, but start climbing gently over a broad crest of grass and heather on **Heptonstall Moor**, around 370m (1215ft).

A boggy patch on the moor may feature bog cotton. The path is generally firm, but soft areas have been paved with flagstones. The whitewashed Pack Horse Inn appears suddenly in view, followed by Gorple Lower Reservoir and its keeper's house. Follow the path gently downhill and walk beside a tumbled wall and fence across a grassy, rushy moor to reach a track and signpost.

The Pennine Way rejoins the Pennine Bridleway at this point. Turn right down through a gate and follow the track down to a stout iron gate leading onto a reservoir access track near the keeper's house. The Pennine Bridleway turns left here, towards Hurstwood, while the reservoir access track can be used to reach a campsite off-route at High Greenwood Farm. The Pennine Way runs straight ahead, down an old stone-paved 'causey' on a grassy, rushy slope to reach a confluence of streams at **Graining Water**.

Cross both streams using footbridges and admire the little bracken-clad valleys with their gritstone edges. Follow the Pennine Way upstream, up another stone-paved 'causey'. A stile on the right can be used to reach the **Pack Horse Inn** for food and drink if desired, otherwise stay on the path through fields and later turn right up to a walled path and a road. This road has summer weekend buses linking Hebden Bridge with Widdop Reservoir.

Turn left along the road to pass Well Hole Cottage. The road leads down to a small car park, where the Pennine Bridleway joins from the left. Walk a little further along the road to find the Pennine Way signposted up to the right. Quickly join a narrow road and turn right to follow it uphill. This passes a small forestry plantation and runs downhill to a junction. Keep left to follow the road uphill again, passing large rushy fields. As the road levels out, a Pennine Way signpost points down to the right.

Cross a stile in a gap in a stout stone wall, then cross the dam of **Walshaw Dean Lower Reservoir**. Turn left, following a firm gravel path and a flagstone path along the grassy, rushy moorland between the shore and a tall stone wall. Note the big house at the head of the reservoir, originally built for the reservoir keeper, extended in recent years. Pass the dam of **Walshaw Dean Middle Reservoir** and pick up a path crossing a metal footbridge.

The first view of the solitary Packhorse Inn, lying a little off-route between Gorple and Walshaw Dean

Top Withins, associated with 'Wuthering Heights', has a basic bothy offering shelter from the weather

Follow an embankment between the reservoir and a stone-built drain. Rhododendron bushes grow along one part of the path, while the opposite shore of the reservoir is completely covered in them. When a stone bridge spans the drain, turn left up a track and go through a gate onto open moorland. Turn right as signposted for the Pennine Way, walking up a slope of grass, heather and rushes. The path is mostly firm, but some softer parts are paved with flagstones. Pass a small memorial on a boulder and later pick up a flagstone path crossing the higher parts of **Withins Height**, around 450m (1475ft). The moor is predominantly grassy and the flagstones run down beside tumbled drystone walls to the ruined farmstead of **Top Withins**.

WUTHERING HEIGHTS

Top Withins has long been associated with Emily Brontë's only novel, *Wuthering Heights*. Despite a disclaimer carved in stone and fixed to the wall of the farm by the Brontë Society, tourists continue to trek up here from Haworth, following signposts in English and Japanese! The ruins have been consolidated and a simple one-roomed bothy has been built alongside.

Map continued on page 72

HAWORTH

It is possible to leave the Pennine Way and walk to Haworth for the night. The path leading across the moors is well-trodden and signposted. A visit offers an opportunity to go to the Brontë Parsonage

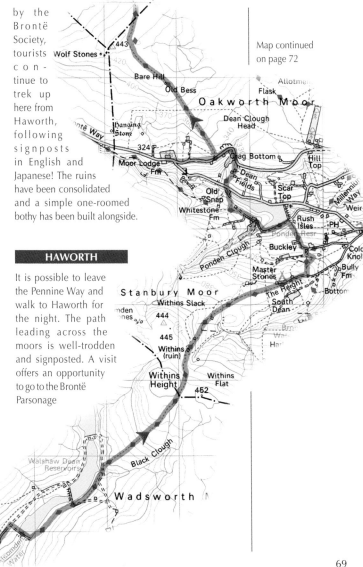

69

Museum, which is open throughout the year (entry charge, tel: 01535 642323, **www.bronte.org.uk**). The village is quaint and attractive and its cobbled main street runs down to the Worth Valley Railway, beloved of steam train buffs, running daily throughout the summer, with a limited winter timetable (tel: 01535 645214, **www.kwvr.co.uk**). A full range of facilities are available in the village, including a tourist information centre (tel: 01535 642329).

Leave **Top Withins** by following a well-worn path and a flagstone path to a signposted junction beside a tumbled ruin. Turning right downhill leads to Haworth, while the Pennine Way keeps straight ahead along a flagstone path. In fact, there are twin lines of flagstones across the moor, allowing access for farm vehicles. Follow these down a rushy slope to cross a stream, then climb past a tree. The track undulates as it traverses moorland criss-crossed by stone walls. Cross a heathery crest and follow the track past **Upper Heights Farm** to reach a signposted junction.

Turning right offers another chance to visit Haworth, but the Pennine Way turns left to pass another house at **Lower Heights**. Watch for a gate and a kissing gate on

Ponden Reservoir, where a few facilities lie just off-route, including a daily bus service to Haworth

the left, signposted for the Pennine Way. The path runs along a broad, grassy swathe flanked by walls, then drops down a moorland slope to reach a track. Turn right to pass houses at **Buckley** then turn sharp left down another track, almost to a house. Turn right beforehand, through a gate and down a path that swings left to reach a road at the dam of **Ponden Reservoir**. ▶

Turn left to follow the road alongside the reservoir, climbing steeply to reach the Ponden Guest House and a basic campsite, near **Ponden Hall**. The hall provided the inspiration for Thrushcross Grange in Emily Brontë's novel *Wuthering Heights*. Climb along a track then head down a tarmac road towards a house. Before reaching it, veer left along a grassy path, and later turn right to the head of Ponden Reservoir to cross a stone-arched bridge.

Turn left along a road, then right over a stone step-stile. Climb straight uphill through fields, watching for marker posts. Climb between a ruin and a restored farm building then walk up its access track. Watch for the Pennine Way signposted left, along a grassy path. Follow it through a couple of gates to reach a road. Turn left to cross a stream and follow the road past a little terrace of houses to reach **Crag Nook Farm**. ▶

Turn sharp right at Crag Nook Farm to follow a winding, grassy, stony track uphill. A gate on the left gives access to a gentle, grassy, rushy moorland slope where a path climbs straight ahead alongside a wall. One stretch has a wall on both sides then a wooden step-stile is crossed. The wall eventually ends very suddenly on **Bare Hill**, but the path winds ahead across a gently rolling moor of grass, bilberry and heather.

A trig point and a small gritstone edge are seen ahead at **Wolf Stones**, but these are not on the route. Pendle Hill and Boulsworth Hill are in view to the left, while the path begins to swing to the right. Cross a heather moor where a flagstone path leads over a crest at 438m (1437ft). Descend gently down the other side, passing a stone shelter before the flagstone path finishes. The path is rough and stony for a while, with views of Pendle Hill,

If you leave the Pennine Way here, a daily bus service can be used to reach the nearby villages of Stanbury or Haworth.

Following the road further leads to a junction, near the furniture showroom of Scartop and its café.

Map continued
from page 69

the southern Yorkshire Dales and a couple of curious monuments perched above Cowling. Another length of flagstones lead to a stone cottage on a dip in the moorland slope. Climb to pass behind this and walk down past four black huts, following a wall on a slope of bilberry and crowberry.

Swing right at the bottom to follow the wall past another hut, then a hut is hidden behind a few trees. After passing one last hut, the path drops to cross a ladder stile beside a gate. Turn left and follow a path between two ruined farmhouses, then cross a footbridge over a stream. Climb across a slope and go through a gate, then walk up a grassy track. Keep right to pass near a farmhouse at **Lumb** and turn round above a small waterfall.

Follow the track up through a gate then when it turns left, keep straight ahead instead. A grassy swathe is flanked by walls and this leads down to a farm. Keep right of the farm buildings, going through little gates to enter and leave the farmyard. Walk straight down through a field to reach a gate onto the A6068 road at **Ickornshaw**. The Pennine Way crosses the road and turns left, but anyone wishing to find accommodation, food and drink should turn right and follow the road into nearby **Cowling**.

COWLING

Facilties in this straggly village are limited to a couple of B&Bs and a basic campsite, as well as a pub, shop and restaurant. A regular daily bus service links with Keighley, Nelson and Burnley.

DAY 5
Ickornshaw to Gargrave

Start	Ickornshaw, Cowling, SD 965 428
Finish	Dalesman Café, Gargrave, SD 931 541
Distance	19km (12 miles)
Ascent	520m (1705ft)
Descent	600m (1970ft)
Maps	OS Landranger 103, OS Explorer OL2 and OL21, Harvey's Pennine Way South
Terrain	Mostly low-lying, but hilly fields are threaded by paths and tracks, with one area of heather moorland. Careful attention to route-finding is required.
Refreshments	Pub at Lothersdale. Pub and café at East Marton. Pubs and a café at Gargrave.

There is a distinct broad gap between the end of the South Pennines and the start of the Yorkshire Dales National Park. Generally referred to as the Aire Gap, this low-lying tract is anything but flat. In fact, it is a roller-coaster of low, grassy drumlin hills, criss-crossed by walls, fences and hedgerows. Careful navigation is required through fields where there may be little or no evidence of a path. There is a stretch of moorland on Pinhaw Beacon, a fine place to look backwards and forwards along the Pennine Way. Strong walkers could reach Gargrave with enough time to spare to press onwards to Malham.

Starting where the Pennine Way crosses the busy A6068 road at **Ickornshaw**, walk towards a furniture showroom called Dovetail, which was formerly the Black Bull pub. Before reaching the building, turn right down a path onto a lower minor road. Turn right again along the road, passing terraced cottages, then turn left up a road and follow it until the tarmac ends. A Pennine Way signpost points along a field path that passes the end of a row of houses at **Middleton**. Shortly afterwards, turn right towards a small huddle of buildings and follow an access track to a minor road.

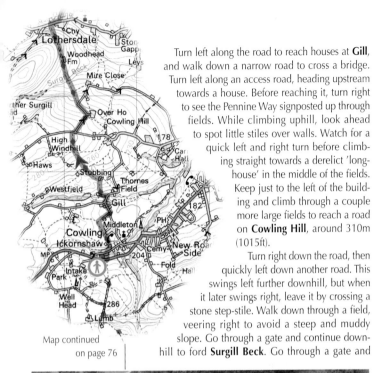

Turn left along the road to reach houses at **Gill**, and walk down a narrow road to cross a bridge. Turn left along an access road, heading upstream towards a house. Before reaching it, turn right to see the Pennine Way signposted up through fields. While climbing uphill, look ahead to spot little stiles over walls. Watch for a quick left and right turn before climbing straight towards a derelict 'long-house' in the middle of the fields. Keep just to the left of the building and climb through a couple more large fields to reach a road on **Cowling Hill**, around 310m (1015ft).

Turn right down the road, then quickly left down another road. This swings left further downhill, but when it later swings right, leave it by crossing a stone step-stile. Walk down through a field, veering right to avoid a steep and muddy slope. Go through a gate and continue downhill to ford **Surgill Beck**. Go through a gate and

Map continued on page 76

The village of Lothersdale, where the biggest waterwheel in England is located inside a mill

climb uphill beside a line of trees that mark the line of an old hedgerow. Walk past **Woodhead Farm** and continue up its access road. When the road begins to head downhill, veer right as signposted to leave it. A path runs down beside a wall, with a charming view of houses nestling in a fold in the hills. Go through a little gate and down a flight of steps to reach a road in **Lothersdale**, and turn right to walk past a pub.

LOTHERSDALE

This charming little village is seen only briefly in passing. Facilities are limited to the Hare and Hounds pub, which offers food and drink, and a basic campsite at Dale End. Hidden from view inside Dale End Mill is the largest water-wheel in England, currently in a poor state of repair. It dates from 1861 and has a diameter of 13.75m (45ft). Hopefully it can be saved.

After passing the pub, turn left up a track and follow it up through a gate. Turn left to climb gently beside a field, then head down into a dip to pass into another field. Climb gently uphill beside the field, turning left at the top to head for a minor road. Cross the road and follow a concrete track gently uphill. When this turns left for **Hewitts Farm**, keep straight ahead through a gate and walk uphill beside a field. Cross a stone step-stile onto heather moorland, following a wall uphill and turning left. When the wall ends at a boggy patch, a firm path climbs open heathery slopes, passing areas of grass, bilberry and bog cotton. A trig point stands on a grassy bump at 388m (1273ft) on **Pinhaw Beacon**. ▶

In clear weather this is a fine viewpoint, looking back to the bleak South Pennines and ahead to the verdant Yorkshire Dales, with Pendle Hill rising prominently between both areas.

Two paths appear to leave the summit; the one to the right is the Pennine Way, though both join together again later. The path broadens and becomes a fine track as it follows a wall down to a road junction. Keep straight ahead and follow the road down **Elslack Moor**. There is a wall on the left, and when this veers left away from the road, follow it to cross a ladder stile beside a gate.

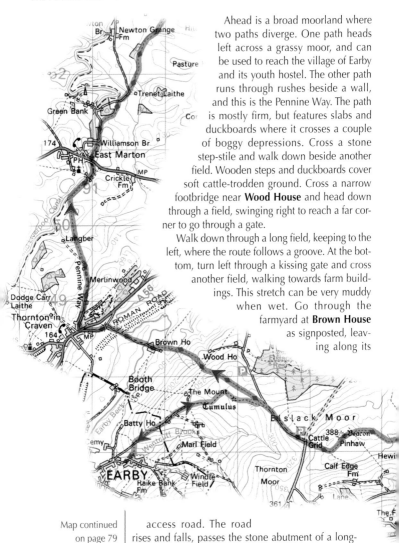

Ahead is a broad moorland where two paths diverge. One path heads left across a grassy moor, and can be used to reach the village of Earby and its youth hostel. The other path runs through rushes beside a wall, and this is the Pennine Way. The path is mostly firm, but features slabs and duckboards where it crosses a couple of boggy depressions. Cross a stone step-stile and walk down beside another field. Wooden steps and duckboards cover soft cattle-trodden ground. Cross a narrow footbridge near **Wood House** and head down through a field, swinging right to reach a far corner to go through a gate.

Walk down through a long field, keeping to the left, where the route follows a groove. At the bottom, turn left through a kissing gate and cross another field, walking towards farm buildings. This stretch can be very muddy when wet. Go through the farmyard at **Brown House** as signposted, leaving along its

Map continued on page 79 access road. The road rises and falls, passes the stone abutment of a long-gone railway bridge then turns left to pass beneath a

Walking along the towpath of the Leeds and Liverpool Canal before East Marton

stone arch. Tall trees line the road as it climbs into the village of **Thornton-in-Craven**. Before the road reaches the busy **A56 road**, a path climbs up a grassy bank, so that the main road can be crossed to reach Cam Lane. There are no facilities beyond bus services to Skipton, Earby, Burnley, Clitheroe and Preston.

Walk up the lane to leave the village, then downhill, then uphill to reach farm buildings. Just after these, turn right and climb diagonally up across a field. Walk down through gates and cross a single-stone 'clam' bridge over a little stream near the house at **Langber**. Walk up through a field and cross a step-stile at the top. Walk downhill, through a gate, and beware a wet and muddy patch on the way up to another gate. Turn right to follow the level towpath of the **Leeds and Liverpool Canal**.

Go under bridge number 160 and pass moorings. Go under the curious double-arched bridge number 161, which carries the busy **A59 road** over the canal. A milepost near the bridge

states 'Leeds 38¼ miles Liverpool 89 miles'. Pass moorings, but don't go under bridge 162, or **Williamson Bridge**. The Pennine Way turns right, away from this bridge, though anyone crossing over it can visit the village of **East Marton**.

EAST MARTON

This little village is charming, but is spoilt by having a busy road running through it. The area near the canal is quiet and the Abbot's Harbour restaurant is available here, with a small food store and campsite. A short walk up the road leads to the Cross Keys pub. Regular daily buses link East Marton with Skipton, Clitheroe and Preston.

The Cross Keys lies just off the Pennine Way in the village of East Marton

Leaving bridge number 162, the Pennine Way runs gently up and down a road. Watch for a gate and signpost on the right, where the route is indicated heading left, diagonally across a field. Watch carefully as the route nips in and out of a patch of woodland, then cross another field to reach a broad track. Turn right to follow

the track, passing the access road for **Trenet Laithe**. Just after the access road, cross a stile on the right and turn left as signposted for the Pennine Way. Walk over a rise and downhill to cross a footbridge, then turn left to walk straight through gently rolling fields, looking ahead and lining up stiles and gates. Cross a track where a left turn could be used to reach nearby accommodation at **Newton Grange**, otherwise keep straight ahead.

The rolling drumlin hills are criss-crossed by fences, while occasional lines of tall trees mark the courses of old hedgerows. A gradual climb onto a hill near **Scaleber** reveals a sudden view of Gargrave ahead, with Cracoe Fell beyond. Head towards the village, following a track only a short way then linking with another track. This heads downhill then climbs over a railway bridge. As it heads downhill again, watch for a gate on the right and pick up a field path to the village of **Gargrave**. Turn left to follow a road past the church and cross the **River Aire**.

GARGRAVE

This is the largest village on the Pennine Way so far, with the best range of services. It stands near the site of a Roman fort, and the church contains fragments of 9th and 10th-century Anglo-Danish crosses. A couple of pubs offer lodgings and there are a couple of river-side B&Bs, as well as a nearby campsite. The famous Dalesman Café has a sign outside reading 'Edale 70 miles Kirk Yetholm 186 miles', but your own distance count may differ. There is also a restaurant and a fish and chip shop, a post office and a few shops, and the Co-op has an ATM. There are trains to Lancaster, Skipton and Leeds, as well as buses to Skipton, Settle and Malham.

Map continued from page 76

79

DAY 6
Gargrave to Malham

Start	Dalesman Café, Gargrave, SD 931 541
Finish	The Green, Malham, SD 901 628
Distance	11km (7 miles)
Ascent	200m (655ft)
Descent	100m (330ft)
Maps	OS Landranger 98 and 103, OS Explorer OL2, Harvey's Pennine Way South
Terrain	Gently rolling grassy hills and easy riverside walks, but keep an eye on the map and look out for signposts and waymarks.
Refreshments	Café off-route at Airton. Pub off-route at Kirkby Malham. Plenty of choice at Malham.

This is a simple and easy half-day walk. Anyone with limited long-distance walking experience might prefer an easy half-day at this stage, after walking for almost a week over rather bleak and exposed moorlands. There is very little climbing on this stage, just a couple of low, grassy hills and a gentle riverside walk. The whole distance could be added to the previous day's walk, but that would leave little time to explore the countryside around Malham. With the afternoon free, a detour can be made from the Pennine Way to visit the awesome limestone gorge of Gordale Scar.

Start at the Dalesman Café in **Gargrave** and walk beside it along West Street. Pass the village hall and keep straight ahead to cross bridge number 170 on the **Leeds and Liverpool Canal** at Higherland Lock. The road is signposted from the canal as the Pennine Way to Malham, but the distance quoted is too short. Walk straight ahead at a junction, along Mark House Lane, passing **Gargrave House** and its Home Farm, surrounded by a tall stone wall.

As the road runs gently uphill watch for a signpost and stone step-stile on the right. Enter a field and turn left to stay low. Do not go into a field ahead containing a barn, but go

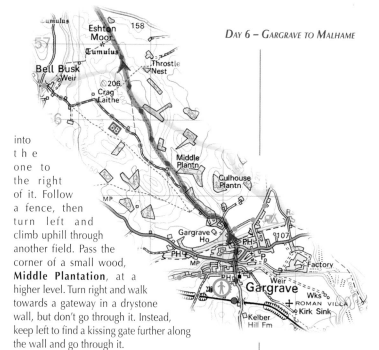

into the one to the right of it. Follow a fence, then turn left and climb uphill through another field. Pass the corner of a small wood, **Middle Plantation**, at a higher level. Turn right and walk towards a gateway in a drystone wall, but don't go through it. Instead, keep left to find a kissing gate further along the wall and go through it.

Cross the next two fields diagonally then bear left to follow a drystone wall to a place where four fields meet. Go through a gate at this point and head diagonally through another field, now walking inside the

Map continued on page 82

A Pennine Way signpost, passed on the descent of Eshton Moor, looking ahead into Airedale

81

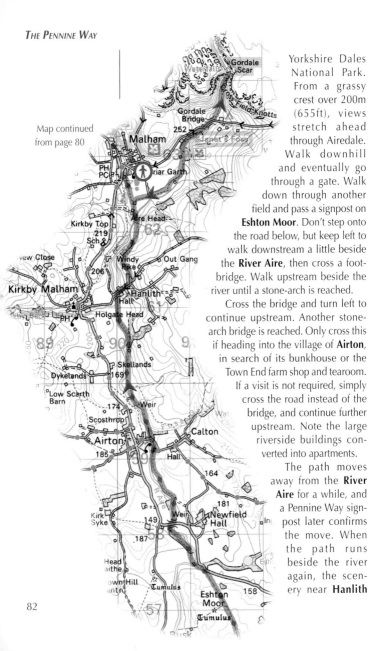

Yorkshire Dales National Park. From a grassy crest over 200m (655ft), views stretch ahead through Airedale. Walk downhill and eventually go through a gate. Walk down through another field and pass a signpost on **Eshton Moor**. Don't step onto the road below, but keep left to walk downstream a little beside the **River Aire**, then cross a foot-bridge. Walk upstream beside the river until a stone-arch is reached.

Cross the bridge and turn left to continue upstream. Another stone-arch bridge is reached. Only cross this if heading into the village of **Airton**, in search of its bunkhouse or the Town End farm shop and tearoom. If a visit is not required, simply cross the road instead of the bridge, and continue further upstream. Note the large riverside buildings converted into apartments.

The path moves away from the **River Aire** for a while, and a Pennine Way sign-post later confirms the move. When the path runs beside the river again, the scenery near **Hanlith**

Map continued from page 80

becomes reminiscent of fine parkland, with tall trees dotted around cattle-grazed pastures. Yet another stone-arch bridge is reached. This can be crossed to reach a pub at Kirkby Malham, but the Pennine Way turns right to climb a steep road, passing **Hanlith Hall** and other former estate buildings.

Sheep graze between tall trees in the riverside parkland below Hanlith Hall

The road bends left, then just as it bends sharp right, step up through a small gate on the left, then cross a field to go through a larger gate. As a path begins to drift downhill, there are brief glimpses of Malham, Malham Cove and Gordale Scar ahead. The path drops through fields to return to the riverside near **Aire Head**. A grassy path climbs gently up to a signposted junction with two hard-surfaced gravel paths. Keep straight ahead to reach the village of **Malham**. Alternatively, consider turning right, off-route along the other path, to visit Janet's Foss and Gordale Scar, which are highly recommended.

MALHAM

As far as possible, try to avoid Malham at busy weekends and holiday periods. The village has a fine range

Walkers stand on a bridge beside a little shop just off the central green in the village of Malham

of facilities but they can come under considerable pressure. Accommodation includes hotels, B&Bs, a youth hostel, bunkhouse and campsites. There are a couple of pubs and cafés as well as a small shop. The National Park Centre, just outside the village, is well worth a visit (open daily April to October, weekends in winter, but closed in January, free entry, tel: 01969 652380). Regular daily buses link Malham with Gargrave and Skipton, and some summer weekend buses run to and from Settle.

Off-route to Gordale Scar

The easiest way to visit to Gordale Scar is to make the detour shortly before reaching Malham. Alternatively, go into the village and leave your pack at your lodgings, then return to pick up the path. There is road access from Malham to Gordale Scar, but it is only 5km (3 miles) there-and-back by footpath.

The path leaving the Pennine Way is signposted for Janet's Foss and passes a barn. The surface is compacted gravel, but after heading through fields towards another barn, the path is made of flagstones. These lead through fields to a third barn, where a stony path proceeds into splendid woodland. There are tall trees, lush undergrowth, and masses of garlic-scented ramsons in spring and early summer. A little waterfall enters a large rock pool at **Janet's Foss**. ◄

Leave the waterfall by walking up a rocky path, taking care on slippery boulders polished like marble. Turn

Geography and geology students are herded here to learn how the river dissolves limestone on one part of its journey, only to deposit some of it elsewhere, notably where the water is agitated. The waterfall at Janet's Foss has deposited a thick mass of lime, known as tufa, where it pours into the rock pool.

Gordale Scar is renowned for its overhanging cliffs and waterfalls and is popular with school groups

right along a road, where there may be a snack van, and reach a broad white path entering **Gordale**. The field near the road is used as a campsite, while beyond, rock walls rear up. Turning a corner, the scene is awesome. **Gordale Scar** is a great cleft with overhanging sides and a boulder-strewn floor. A waterfall pours from a hole in a rock face, cascading into the gorge, leaving thick masses of tufa that have cemented all loose rocks into one chaotic mass. When your senses have had their fill, retrace your steps to Malham.

DAY 7
Malham to Horton in Ribblesdale

Start	The Green, Malham, SD 901 628
Finish	Pen-y-Ghent Café, Horton in Ribblesdale, SD 808 725
Distance	24km (15 miles)
Ascent	810m (2660ft)
Descent	780m (2560ft)
Maps	OS Landranger 98, OS Explorer OL2, Harvey's Pennine Way South
Terrain	Short green grass and limestone pavement around Malham gives way to high moorland on Fountains Fell. Steep rock-steps are climbed on Pen-y-Ghent, followed by a descent on a firm path and a rough and stony track.
Refreshments	The famous Pen-y-Ghent Café is at Horton, along with two pubs.

After a gentle couple of days, allowing walkers to build up their stamina, the Pennine Way heads for the hills again. Malham Cove is a remarkable cliff seen to good effect at the start of the day, while Malham Tarn is seen later. Fountains Fell is climbed and is the highest point gained so far along the Pennine Way, but it is quickly followed by the ascent of Pen-y-Ghent, which is even higher. The climb to the summit is one of the steepest and rockiest parts of the trail. A long descent leads to the straggly village of Horton in Ribblesdale, where the famous Pen-y-Ghent Café has been open almost as long as the Pennine Way.

Follow the road from **Malham** towards Malham Cove, maybe taking a look inside the National Trust's Town Head Barn, just before reaching a campsite. Just after the campsite, pick up a firm path on the right and follow it through fields, noting the rumpled lines of ancient field boundaries along the way. The curved cliff face of **Malham Cove** looms ahead. Either walk to its base then double back, or turn left beforehand to climb a long flight of stone steps. At the top, turn right to walk across limestone pavement close to the cliff edge. Turn left only when the grassy green velvet floor of a valley is seen.

MALHAM COVE

Rising sheer for 70m (230ft), and even overhanging in places, Malham Cove attracts rock climbers, walkers and those who simply stand and stare. The rock is limestone, notable for being riddled with fissures and caves through which water flows. A stream issues from the base of the cliff, but at the end of the Ice Age, when the fissures in the limestone were partly waterlogged and partly blocked by clay, a river poured over the rim of the cliff. This was 'taller than Niagara Falls,' as teachers often say to impress their students, but the volume of water and the overall impact would have been considerably less.

Leave the top of Malham Cove by walking along the grassy floor of a valley, with a line of little cliffs rising on either side. A drystone wall runs all the way, leading to a rugged flight of stone steps at the head of the valley. Turn sharp right at the top to follow a path across a slope then walk beside a little gorge, noting a cave in the cliff opposite. Further up the valley a river is reached. In wet weather it flows further down the valley than in dry weather, but no matter how

Map continued on page 91

The remarkable amphitheatre cliff of Malham Cove can be inspected from bottom to top

much if flows, it always vanishes into its own bed at the **Water Sinks**.

WATER SINKS

It seems fair to assume that the water flowing from Malham Tarn, draining into the Water Sinks, is the same water that flows from the base of Malham Cove. This is not the case. Fluorescent dye was poured down the Water Sinks in the 1960s, and later surfaced at Aire Head, south of Malham village. The water at the base of Malham Cove actually has its source further west.

A road is reached near the Water Sinks. Turn right and follow it across the river and through a gate. Turn left through a car park and follow a path over a grassy rise to see the outflow of **Malham Tarn**. Keep to the right of the tarn, and later keep to the right of a wall enclosing woodland, to reach a track. Turn left and follow the track through a gate. The track runs close to Malham Tarn then it climbs through a wood to reach **Malham Tarn House**.

MALHAM TARN

All the rock in view around Malham Tarn is permeable limestone, so the presence of so much water is curious. In fact, the bed of the tarn is ancient Silurian slate, impermeable to water. The tarn had its level raised by a small dam and Malham Tarn House was built as a shooting lodge. The whole area is a National Nature Reserve, featuring uncommon plants in a lime-rich fen, woodlands rich in willow and ash, with a rampant understorey. The tarn itself attracts a variety of birds. The area is owned by the National Trust, but the house is leased to the Field Studies Council, which runs a variety of courses in the area (tel: 01729 830331, **www.field-studies-council. org**, or pick up information while passing).

Follow the track round the back of Malham Tarn House, then head downhill through a rock cutting, passing a viewpoint overlooking Malham Tarn. Emerge from the woods at **Water Houses** and turn right through a gate. A broad green path follows a drystone wall, rising and falling through a gentle fold in the hills, passing from field to field. Keep to the right of a barn then keep well to the right of two more barns close together. Cross a ladder stile beside a tree, then walk downhill and turn left down to a gate and stone step-stile. Turn right as signposted up to a junction of a minor road and a track.

Follow the track towards **Tennant Gill**, but keep left of the farm buildings and enclosing wall. Climb straight up a broad, grassy path and cross a stone step-stile beside a gate. Turn left across a moorland slope, then right to follow a tumbled drystone wall up a slope of grass, sedge and rushes. The gradient eases in an area of sink holes, where the path swings right, away from the tumbled wall, crossing a gentle dip to ford the little stream of **Tennant Gill**.

Go through a gate in a wall and follow the path onwards, which has been resurfaced across a boggy slope, but can still be muddy in wet weather. The path climbs, but it also drops a little later, then it climbs more consistently over grass and bilberry moors, with heather and bog cotton at a higher level. Gradients are gentle on top of **Fountains Fell**. The highest point isn't visited and a sign warns against leaving the path, as there are open mineshafts dotted around. Most walkers are content to step to the right to reach two tall cairns, over 650m (2135ft), and enjoy the views from there.

FOUNTAINS FELL

The name of the fell derives from its former owners, the distant Fountains Abbey. Huge areas of the Yorkshire Dales were divided between monasteries and used for sheep-grazing. The broad moorland top was mined for coal and is dotted with bell pits. Flagstones were also quarried, leaving hummocky spoil heaps, ample building material for a wall snaking across the summit, with enough left over for a variety of cairns. The view takes

Broken flagstones on top of Fountains Fell provide the material for a tall cairn

in the famous Three Peaks of Yorkshire – Ingleborough, Pen-y-Ghent and Whernside. Buckden Pike and Great Whernside are among other prominent heights in view.

The Pennine Way crosses a stone step-stile to leave Fountains Fell. It drops down a steep slope, passing a fine rocky outcrop at one point. The path surface is rough and stony at first, but some lower parts are pleasant and grassy, slicing down across a steep and rushy slope. A prominent groove runs down to a wall and the wall leads down through a gate to a minor road. Turn left to cross a cattle grid and follow the road gently uphill past a farm at **Rainscar**, hidden among trees. Follow the road across another cattle grid then turn

Map continued
on page 93

right along a track leading to a farm at **Dale Head**.

Keep right of the farm to follow the track through a field and over rolling, grassy, rushy moorland. When a junction is reached at the prominent deep pit of **Churn Milk Hole**, turn right

Anyone daunted by the appearance of the slope can short-cut down to Horton in Ribblesdale.

and keep climbing. There is some heather on the moor then a duckboard runs across a stretch of boggy ground. A firm path leads up to a stone step-stile at a junction of walls. Follow the path alongside a wall, along a rushy crest, heading towards the rugged southern end of Pen-y-Ghent. ◀

Climb up a stone-pitched path with rugged steps, which gives way to an intriguing flight of natural limestone steps. The path levels out on a shelf dividing the limestone from gritstone bedrock. Climb up another stone-pitched path, which gives way to natural, chunky gritstone steps. A broad and obvious path leads to the trig point on the summit of **Pen-y-Ghent** at 694m (2277ft).

PEN-Y-GHENT

This is the lowest of the famous Three Peaks of Yorkshire, yet it offers an extensive view. Distant Pendle Hill and the Bowland Fells are followed by close neighbours Ingleborough and Whernside. The Howgill Fells, Baugh Fell and Wild Boar Fell are followed by High Seat and Great Shunner Fell. Rogan's Seat is followed by a rather vague skyline of moorlands, leading the eye to the shapely Buckden Pike, Great Whernside and Fountains Fell, with Pikedaw Hill completing the panorama.

Cross one of two stiles over the wall, noting how stone seats have been built to mirror each other on either side of the wall. Walk away from the wall, down a rugged stony path. When a steep edge is reached, swing right to follow it, and note the transition from gritstone back onto limestone. Looking ahead, spot a pinnacle of rock standing out from a limestone cliff face. The path swings left and is firm underfoot as it drops down a boggy, rushy slope. Cross a dip where there is heather on the moor, then go through a gate to continue downhill. Cross a gentle, rushy rise, but note that **Hunt Pot** could be visited just off-route. Go through another gate, cross a dip and turn left through yet another gate. Alternatively, turn right to detour to **Hull Pot**.

HUNT POT AND HULL POT

The limestone slopes of Pen-y-Ghent are riddled with caves. Many have been explored in great detail, but many more are too narrow to enter. Hunt Pot and Hull Pot lie close to the Pennine Way, and both of them swallow streams. The waterfall pouring into Hunt Pot later emerges at Douk Gill Scar, while the water seeping into the bouldery bed of Hull Pot emerges at Brants Gill Head. Both resurgences are near Horton in Ribblesdale.

A broad and stony walled track leads off the moors, undulating, but generally descending, and rather awkward underfoot in places. There is an attractive rugged valley down to the left at first, then later fields on both sides, and a patch of woodland is passed later. When a junction is reached, turn right to descend to a road in the middle of **Horton in Ribblesdale**. The Pennine Way turns right along the road to pass the Pen-y-Ghent Café. If it is open, go in and sign the Pennine Way visitor book, adding your name to countless thousands of others amassed over forty-odd years.

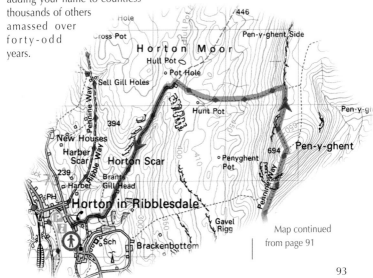

Map continued
from page 91

The church at Horton in Ribblesdale has some Norman features, but is mostly 15th century

HORTON IN RIBBLESDALE

It takes time to walk from one end of this straggly village to the other, and anyone wishing to head straight for their lodgings should ensure they are heading in the right direction! Horton's accommodation includes B&Bs, bunkhouse and a campsite. There are a couple of pubs and a shop, along with the celebrated Pen-y-Ghent Café. The café also serves as a tourist information centre (tel: 01729 860333). Occasional buses run between Horton and Settle, while daily trains run along the celebrated Settle to Carlisle railway, straight through the heart of the Yorkshire Dales.

DAY 8
Horton in Ribblesdale to Hawes

Start	Pen-y-Ghent Café, Horton in Ribblesdale, SD 808 725
Finish	Town Centre, Hawes, SD 873 898
Distance	24km (15 miles)
Ascent	490m (1610ft)
Descent	490m (1610ft)
Maps	OS Landranger 98, OS Explorer OL2, Harvey's Pennine Way Central
Terrain	Mostly long tracks, running at gentle gradients among rolling hills or across moorland slopes. The highest part is a narrow tarmac road. Keep an eye on signposts and marker posts when following paths linking these tracks.
Refreshments	Plenty of choice around Hawes.

This looks like a long day on maps, because most of the distance is made up of direct old packhorse ways. While there are plenty of ups and downs along these tracks, the overall gradient is uphill for the first half of the day, then downhill for the second half. The countryside is remarkably interesting, honeycombed with caves, and the entrances to some of these can be studied. There is a National Nature Reserve at Ling Gill, where a rocky gorge is full of trees and plants. Cam High Road, followed in the middle of the day, is one of the highest Roman roads in Britain. During the final descent, care is needed to follow an intricate route between the village of Gayle and the bustling little market town of Hawes.

Start from the Pen-y-Ghent Café in **Horton in Ribblesdale** and follow the road to The Crown. Turn right and then left through the pub car park to pick up and follow a track uphill, flanked by drystone walls. Go through a gate. The wall on the right later peters out, and the track undulates across grassy hills while climbing to another gate. Just before this gate, note the **Sell Gill Holes** on the right. ▶

This is an entertaining little cave, having 'wet' and 'dry' entrances. Access requires rigging up a rope or a ladder. After descending three pitches there is a final large chamber.

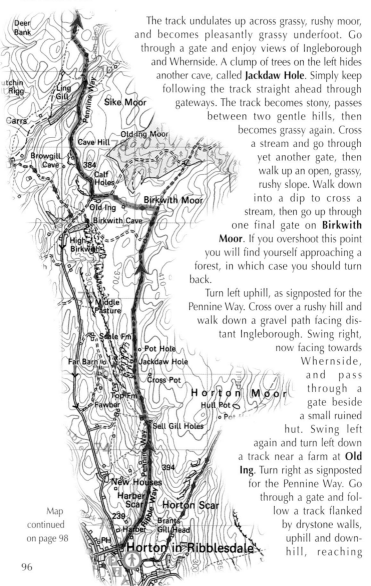

The track undulates up across grassy, rushy moor, and becomes pleasantly grassy underfoot. Go through a gate and enjoy views of Ingleborough and Whernside. A clump of trees on the left hides another cave, called **Jackdaw Hole**. Simply keep following the track straight ahead through gateways. The track becomes stony, passes between two gentle hills, then becomes grassy again. Cross a stream and go through yet another gate, then walk up an open, grassy, rushy slope. Walk down into a dip to cross a stream, then go up through one final gate on **Birkwith Moor**. If you overshoot this point you will find yourself approaching a forest, in which case you should turn back.

Turn left uphill, as signposted for the Pennine Way. Cross over a rushy hill and walk down a gravel path facing distant Ingleborough. Swing right, now facing towards Whernside, and pass through a gate beside a small ruined hut. Swing left again and turn left down a track near a farm at **Old Ing**. Turn right as signposted for the Pennine Way. Go through a gate and follow a track flanked by drystone walls, uphill and downhill, reaching

Map
continued
on page 98

A heavily-laden Pennine Wayfarer calls a halt near Jackdaw Hole and lets others forge ahead

another gate where the **Calf Holes** can be inspected on the right. ▶

Follow the track onwards, passing a barn and noting little groups of mature trees dotted around the fields. The track runs alongside the National Nature Reserve of **Ling Gill**, a rock-walled gorge full of dense woodland. The stream feeding into it, **Cam Beck**, is crossed using an old stone packhorse bridge bearing a tablet with indecipherable lettering, but dating from 1765.

Follow the track onwards up a grassy, rushy moor. At a higher level, when views are more extensive, there is a feeling of being embraced by the Three Peaks of Yorkshire. Turn right at a junction of tracks at 438m (1437ft) on **Cam End**, and keep climbing gradually. The track is called Cam High Road and is based on an old Roman road, later restored as a packhorse way, used as part of the Dales Way, and resurfaced in recent years.

Go through a gate in a wall, looking down on the extensive forest of Cam Woodlands. Keep climbing gradually, passing a cairn and signpost where the Dales Way descends across a moorland slope to reach Cam Houses.

This cave is often visited by novices, but the initial descent into the cave requires a rope or a ladder. After wading through a flooded passage, there is a flat-out crawl to endure. A walkable passage leads to an exit at the nearby Browgill Cave.

The track, however, keeps climbing and passes through a gate. Further along, the track joins the access track rising from Cam Houses, and the Pennine Way continues straight ahead along a narrow tarmac road. There is a dip in the road where a gate is passed, then the road rolls gently across a high limestone pasture at 572m (1877ft). Before the

Map continued on page 100

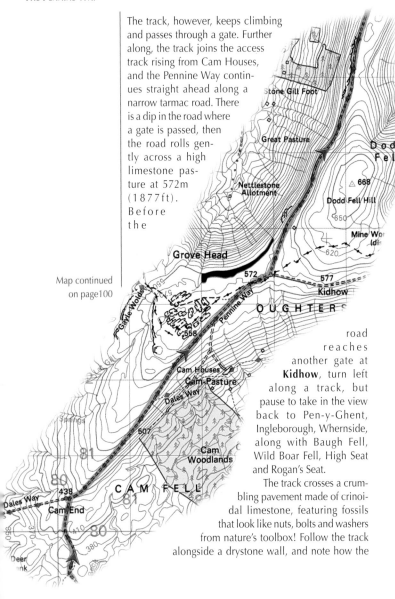

road reaches another gate at **Kidhow**, turn left along a track, but pause to take in the view back to Pen-y-Ghent, Ingleborough, Whernside, along with Baugh Fell, Wild Boar Fell, High Seat and Rogan's Seat.

The track crosses a crumbling pavement made of crinoidal limestone, featuring fossils that look like nuts, bolts and washers from nature's toolbox! Follow the track alongside a drystone wall, and note how the stones in the wall change from limestone, to sandstone, and later back to limestone, reflecting the rock types underfoot. The track traverses at around 580m (1900ft) across the slopes of **Dodd Fell**. Limestone pavement again shows through before the track heads downhill.

Watch for a signpost on the right, where the Pennine Way leaves the track and instead heads up a green grassy path at **Ten End**. ▸ The path levels out, passing a quarried rock-step and a few sinkholes, following a tumbled wall onwards. Go through a gate and wind downhill on a grassy path. Walk along a moorland shelf strewn with gritstone boulders, then head down to a corner formed by drystone walls to go through a gate. Walk downhill beside a wall on a moorland slope of grass, sedge and rushes. It can be squelchy underfoot at **Backsides**, and the path heads from gate to gate, down past **Gaudy House**. Join a minor road and walk downhill past fields.

The track can be used to make a direct descent to Hawes.

When a road junction is reached, first turn right, then left as signposted for the Pennine Way, and go through a tiny gate and gap stile. A path leads onwards, down through two fields, then turn left to walk down through

Extensive meadows of buttercups on the way down from the moors into Wensleydale

two more fields to reach another minor road. Turn right along this road, but quickly turn left down into the little village of **Gayle**. The Pennine Way is signposted on left, following a flagstone path through two fields. Walk along a narrow path through a housing estate, crossing over one road to reach another road.

Turn left along the road, then right as signposted along a path. A fine flagstone path leads over to a church. Turn right at a junction beside the church and walk down another flagstone path into **Hawes**. Turn left at

Map continued from page 98

the White Hart Inn to reach the town centre.

HAWES

This popular and busy little market town has many points of interest and is well worth exploring. Attractions include the Dales Countryside Museum, open daily, but closed in January (entry charge, tel: 01969 666210). The museum shares the old railway station site with the National Park Centre (tel: 01969 666210). The Wensleydale

The Dales Countryside Museum is located at the old railway station buildings in Hawes

Creamery reminds visitors that the first Wensleydale cheese was made in the dale by Cistercian monks in 1150. The creamery is open daily throughout the year (tel: 01969 667664, **www.wensleydale.co.uk**).

Hawes has the greatest range of services so far along the Pennine Way, including banks with ATMs, a post office, shops, pubs, restaurants, cafés and a fish and chip shop. A range of accommodation includes hotels, B&Bs, a youth hostel and a campsite. Regular daily buses run through Wensleydale, linking Hawes with Leyburn. Another bus service links Hawes with Garsdale Station on the celebrated Settle to Carlisle railway. A limited summer Sunday bus links Hawes with Leeds.

DAY 9

Hawes to Keld

Start	Town Centre, Hawes, SD 873 898
Finish	Park Lodge, Keld, NY 892 012
Distance	21km (13 miles)
Ascent	715m (2345ft)
Descent	615m (2020ft)
Maps	OS Landranger 91 and 98, OS Explorer OL19 and 30, Harvey's Pennine Way Central
Terrain	The bulk of the day's walk involves a long and gradual ascent and descent over a broad moorland crest. Boggy parts feature flagstone paths, but this is an exposed place in bad weather. The latter part of the route involves contouring round a steep hillside on a rugged path.
Refreshments	Pub and café at Hardraw, Thwaite and Keld.

The Pennine Way runs through fields between Hawes and Hardraw, and before walking any further, a highly recommended detour allows Hardraw Force to be visited. Don't be put off if there is heavy rain, since the waterfall will be at its most powerful. A long and gradual climb leads up a broad moorland crest over Great Shunner Fell. In mist, the climb is a treadmill and there is a succession of 'false' summits, but on a clear day the walk is delightful and views are exceptionally wide-ranging. The descent to Thwaite offers fine views of Swaledale, as does the continuation round the steep slopes of Kisdon, on the way to the charming village of Keld.

Leave the centre of **Hawes** by following the road signposted for the Dales Countryside Museum. The Pennine Way is signposted left before the turning for the museum and tourist information centre. The road crosses an old railway bridge and a steam train can be seen alongside the old station building. Walk down the road a little then when another road leads off to the left, the Pennine Way is signposted straight along a flagstone path through a

Hardraw Force is well worth a short detour, especially after a spell of heavy rain

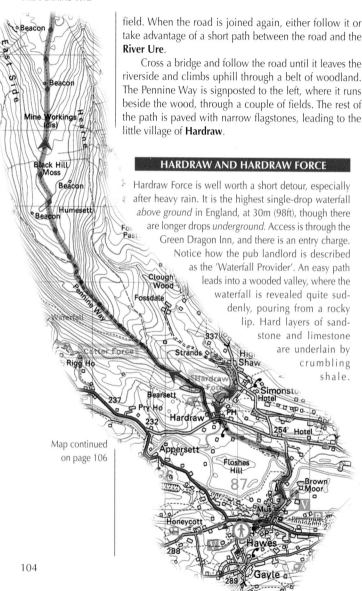

field. When the road is joined again, either follow it or take advantage of a short path between the road and the **River Ure**.

Cross a bridge and follow the road until it leaves the riverside and climbs uphill through a belt of woodland. The Pennine Way is signposted to the left, where it runs beside the wood, through a couple of fields. The rest of the path is paved with narrow flagstones, leading to the little village of **Hardraw**.

HARDRAW AND HARDRAW FORCE

Hardraw Force is well worth a short detour, especially after heavy rain. It is the highest single-drop waterfall *above ground* in England, at 30m (98ft), though there are longer drops *underground*. Access is through the Green Dragon Inn, and there is an entry charge. Notice how the pub landlord is described as the 'Waterfall Provider'. An easy path leads into a wooded valley, where the waterfall is revealed quite suddenly, pouring from a rocky lip. Hard layers of sandstone and limestone are underlain by crumbling shale.

Map continued on page 106

Charles Blondin, the 19th-century tightrope walker, crossed the gorge and stopped halfway to cook an omelette! The lip of the waterfall collapsed in 1899, but the rock was pinned with iron bars to restore the waterfall to its former glory.

Facilities at Hardraw include the Green Dragon Inn, which provides food, drink, accommodation, bunkhouse and a campsite. The nearby Cart House tearoom also runs a campsite. A bus service links Hardraw with Hawes and Garsdale Station.

The Pennine Way runs along the road from the pub, past the tearoom, to reach the edge of **Hardraw**. Turn right as signposted along a walled track, passing a house, climbing past fields and a woodland, crossing a gentle hump to reach a gate onto the open moors. Fork left at a track junction and climb up a grassy, rushy crest with increasingly wide-ranging views. Climb further and pass a wall, and notice how the bedrock varies from sandstone to limestone. Go through a gate in a wall, where the track is worn down to the limestone bedrock.

Walk a short way up the track then turn right as signposted for the Pennine Way. A broad and grassy path rises gently along a broad moorland crest. Some parts may be squelchy underfoot after rain. A series of cairns mark the way ahead, which are useful guides in mist. Gritstone boulders are dotted around on the way to and from a low gritstone edge bearing a prominent cairn at **Humesett**. Other tall, columnar cairns standing on the moorland slopes are referred to as 'beacons'.

The path is worn down to gritstone bedrock, which forms a natural paved surface. Later, there is a stretch of redundant wooden duckboard. The path stays on the high crest, generally following a firm, sandy path. A broad and gentle dip in the crest at **Black Hill Moss** features peat hags, and a flagstone path provides a firm footing. ▶

Longer stretches of flagstones follow the grassy crest and a bog pool stands on the left. Climb a stony, grassy path, which levels out, then flagstones cross another slight dip on the crest. A stony path climbs to a prominent cairn,

Watch the ground while crossing a rocky little streambed to see marks that look remarkably like tyre tracks. These are actually the imprints of ancient fossil trees, such as lepidodendron or sigillaria, which could grow as tall as 40m (130ft). See picture on page 17.

or **beacon**. Follow a level path along a broad crest then use a flagstone path to cross a slight depression where the boggy ground features grass and bilberry. Climb gently up a firm path, which alternates between a stony surface and flagstones, though another slight depression features a longer stretch of flagstones, with bog cotton alongside. A steeper slope is equipped with stone steps, then the path undulates up and down stone-slab steps among peat hags and boggy patches. The path is firm and dry along a high crest, crossing a step-stile over a fence to reach a stone cross-shelter on top of **Great Shunner Fell** at 716m (2349ft).

GREAT SHUNNER FELL

This is the highest point gained so far on the Pennine Way. In the past the broad whaleback crest featured appalling bogs, and in wet and misty weather the climb seemed endless. When available, the view is remarkably extensive. Look along the Vale of Eden, with Cross Fell, the Dun Fells, Mickle Fell and the North Pennines rising above it. Closer to hand are Rogan's Seat and Swaledale, along with the eastern parts of the Yorkshire Dales. Great Whernside and Buckden Pike lead the eye to Fountains Fell and Pen-y-Ghent, with the Bowland Fells more distant. Ingleborough, Whernside and Gragareth are followed by Baugh Fell. The distant skyline of the Lake District includes the Coniston Fells, Scafells, Helvellyn and High Street ranges, followed by Skiddaw and Blencathra. Closer at hand are Wild Boar Fell, High Seat and Nine Standards Rigg.

Map continued on page 108

Follow a paved path away from the shelter and cross another step-stile over a fence. The path descends and undulates, passing a stout cairn, or **beacon**, and crossing a footbridge at one point. There is a break in the flagstone path while crossing a grassy hump, then another long and undulating paved path continues. A stony path and a flagstone path lead down to a prominent little spoil heap where coal was once mined. Walk down another stony path and another flagstone path.

Turn left to follow a stony track to a gate, enjoying fine views along the length of Swaledale, taking note of all its field barns. These are so numerous that almost every field has its own barn. The track is flanked by dry-stone walls and leads to the **B6270 road**. Turn right to follow the road down into the little village of **Thwaite**. In a word, Kearton's supplies all your needs here, offering a hotel, tea shop and provisions to take away.

Walk through the village by road, but watch for a Pennine Way signpost on the left. Walk through a couple of little fields, then turn left and go through a gate. Cross a field and a stream, then go through another gate and turn right. The path climbs uphill then a level, grassy track leads to a farm at **Kisdon**. Go through a gate at the farm and immediately turn left as signposted up through another gate, to follow a broad path flanked by drystone

The long and gradual climb onto Great Shunner Fell is hampered by 'false summits' along the way

A 'beacon' cairn on the way down Great Shunner Fell, with a view into the lovely Swaledale

walls. When a building is reached, keep left above it, then follow a path running more or less level, with fine views along Swaledale.

The path drifts downhill and when a junction is reached, fork right downhill. Traverse boulder-scree on the slopes of **Kisdon** and be thankful that a path has been made through it, although some parts are still uneven underfoot. Cross a steep slope of bracken above a wood predominantly planted with birch trees. There is a tumbled wall alongside the wood, and after following it for a while, step down through a gap in the wall, and later keep left to maintain a falling traverse.

A signpost is reached, where the Pennine Way makes a sharp right turn downhill. If you wish to continue directly towards Tan Hill, then turn right. Visiting **Keld** requires a short detour off-route, straight ahead along a clear path. The village is reached at its lowest point, beside Park Lodge.

KELD

Keld is a delightful little village, full of stout stone houses and of no great size. Anyone breaking here will probably have time to wander around and explore, and if so, then it is worth taking a stroll beside the River Swale. Kisdon Force lies downstream while Catrake Force and Wain Wath Force lie upstream.

Facilities in Keld include a hotel, a couple of B&Bs, a bunkhouse and a campsite. There is a small shop and café at Park Lodge. Bear in mind that the Pennine Way and the Coast to Coast Walk cross over each other at Keld, which puts a lot of pressure on the limited accommodation. If lodgings cannot be secured, then press onwards to the Tan Hill Inn. An occasional bus service allows walkers to move off-route in search of other lodgings in Swaledale.

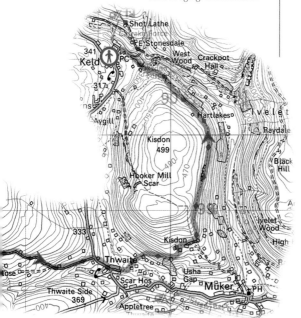

Map continued from page 106

DAY 10
Keld to Baldersdale or Bowes

Start	Park Lodge, Keld, NY 892 012
Finish	Clove Lodge, Baldersdale, NY 935 177
Alternative finish	St Giles' Church, Bowes, NY 993 135
Distance	24km (15 miles); alternative 20km (12½ miles)
Ascent	400m (1310ft); alternative 250m (820ft)
Descent	400m (1310ft); alternative 300m (985ft)
Maps	OS Landranger 91, OS Explorer OL30 and OL31, Harvey's Pennine Way Central
Terrain	Broad and open moorland slopes, which might be wet on the way to Tan Hill, and are wet and boggy beyond Tan Hill, most of the way to Baldersdale. On the alternative route, fiddly field paths lead to Bowes.
Refreshments	The Tan Hill Inn, the highest pub in England. A pub is available on the alternative route at Bowes.

After leaving Keld, the Pennine Way climbs towards Tan Hill and its celebrated inn. Many walkers structure their schedules so that they can stay at the inn, or camp alongside. Beyond Tan Hill is the bleak and boggy Stainmore, where the Pennine Way splits into 'main' and 'alternative' routes, which later join again in Baldersdale. There was once a youth hostel at Baldersdale, but since it closed there is only a solitary farmhouse B&B. If it is full and you cannot face the long walk to Middleton-in-Teesdale, then you should consider taking the alternative route to Bowes. Both routes have their pros and cons, so read both descriptions carefully before making a choice. It is also possible to walk to Bowes and still stay at Clove Lodge!

Leave **Keld** by following a path downhill from Park Lodge. When a fork is reached, this is where the Pennine Way comes in on the right from Thwaite, and continues down on the left to reach a footbridge over the **River Swale**. Cross over and follow a path uphill, but take the time to look down on the lovely waterfall of East Gill Force. The path climbs steeply to a track, and a left turn leads up to some farm buildings at **East Stonesdale**.

Pass between the buildings and climb straight up through a gate to follow a grassy path flanked by drystone walls. This leads up to a gate, then the route passes to the right of a barn at **Shot Lathe**, onto a grassy, rushy open space beyond. Keep climbing and look back to Keld one last time. Go through a gate and note that the rushy moor can be squelchy, but drier heather moorland lies further ahead. Go through another gate and follow the path as it undulates across a moorland slope of grass, sedge and rushes. Pass well below a farmhouse at **Frith Lodge** and go through a little gate.

Join and follow a track straight ahead, keeping right of a barn. Go through a gate and follow a firm gravel track towards two more barns. Go through gates to pass these and cross a little stream. Walk straight along a broad path on the wet, rushy, grassy moorland slopes of **Low Brown Hill**. The path appears to drift down towards a minor road and a couple of bridges over Stonesdale Beck, so swing right and cross a stone-slab footbridge over **Lad Gill**.

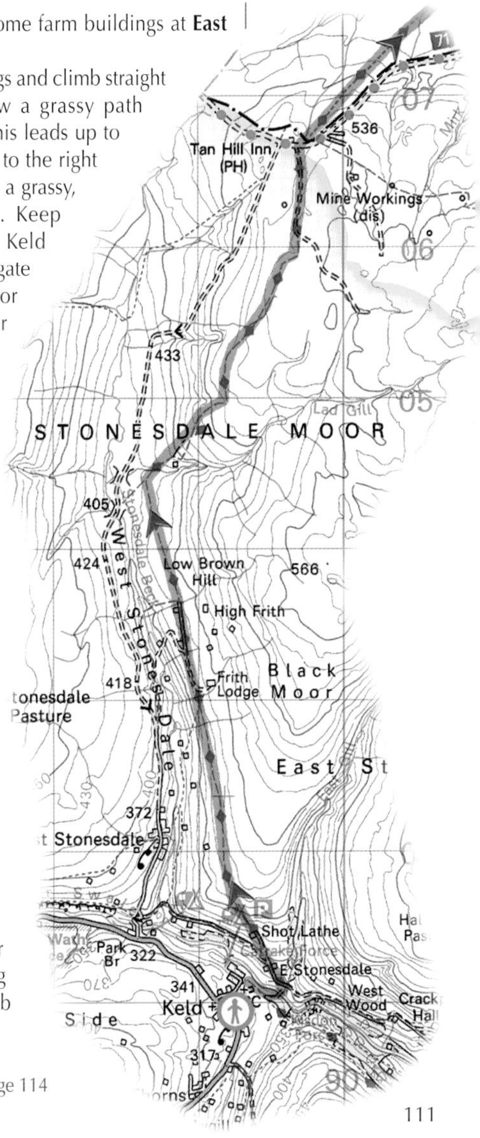

Map continued on page 114

111

The Tan Hill Inn is the highest pub in England, offering a range of services at 530m (1732ft)

The path climbs up onto **Stonesdale Moor** and becomes a stony track, levelling out among grass, sedge and rushes. Keep right at a fork, as signposted for the Pennine Way. There is a gentle rise along another old track, passing the spoil heap of an old coal mine. The Tan Hill Inn suddenly comes into view at this point. The track swings right, but two signposts send it left and left again along a broad, clear, stony track. Join a road literally at the front door of the **Tan Hill Inn**. The road marks the end of the Yorkshire Dales National Park and the start of the extensive North Pennines Area of Outstanding Natural Beauty.

THE TAN HILL INN

The Tan Hill Inn is the highest pub in England, standing at a lonely moorland road junction at 530m (1732ft). William Camden mentioned an inn at this remote spot in 1586, but the current structure dates from the 17th century. The inn stood at a focal point on packhorse ways and caught the passing trade. Bell pits and open mine shafts dot the bleak moors, and coal mining provided a more regular clientele. There is good local support for the inn but it relies heavily on tourist traffic, and Pennine Wayfarers seldom pass if the doors are open.

Tan Hill Inn was 'transferred' to County Durham during the local government reorganisation of April 1974, and this was a sore point with many locals. It was brought back into Yorkshire following a boundary change in April 1991. The pub has featured in television advertising to promote double-glazing, and in foul weather a blazing fire should be burning, but there may be competition for a fireside seat! A variety of accommodation is available, from B&B to bunkhouse and camping (tel: 01833 628246, **www.tanhillinn.com**).

To leave the Tan Hill Inn, follow the road towards a nearby cattle grid. Turn left just beforehand to cross a wooden step-stile over a fence. A firm, grassy path descends where the bedrock is limestone, then the bleak and boggy **Sleightholme Moor** begins. Grass, sedge and rushes give way to heather. Follow white-tipped marker posts gently downhill. The moor can be wet, especially where bare, black peat or bright green sphagnum moss is seen. The gradient is almost level and the path runs well to the left of a drystone sheepfold. The course of **Frumming Beck** is followed downstream. The route runs along the northern bank, where it was transferred after the southern bank was trodden into a miserable morass.

Simply keep the beck in view while following it downstream, generally walking on a brow some distance from the flow. There are a couple of little footbridges over inflowing streams, then a stout pepperpot cairn is passed. Another little footbridge is followed by a few lengths of duckboard, and two more sheepfolds stand away to the right. The path gets better and better along a brow of grass and sedge, eventually drifting down to a track.

Turn right to cross a bridge and walk up the track, passing a barrier gate to reach a junction. Turn left along a broad, stony track over moorland of rushes and sedge,

A fine track runs parallel to Sleightholme Beck, becoming a road as it reaches Sleightholme Farm

now running parallel to Sleightholme Beck, though high above the flow. The track undulates and is part gravel and part patchy tarmac, eventually running down through a gate to pass **Sleightholme Farm**. Follow the farm road past fields to pass a converted barn at Kingdom Lodge.

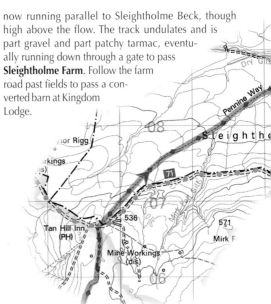

Turn left through a gate, as signposted for the Pennine Way, and aim straight for another gate to pass from field to field. A layered, crumbling cliff is seen ahead, so aim to the right of it to go through another gate and cross a footbridge over **Sleightholme Beck**. Turn right, but almost immediately fork left up a grassy path. Walk roughly parallel to a wall along a brow covered in rushes and bracken, then go through a gate on the left. Turn right to continue following the wall towards a farmhouse at **Trough Heads**. A three-way Pennine Way signpost

Map continued on page 117

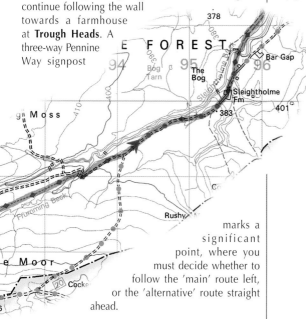

marks a significant point, where you must decide whether to follow the 'main' route left, or the 'alternative' route straight ahead.

Main route

Turn left, as signposted for God's Bridge, and walk across the heathery **Wytham Moor**, spiked with patches of rushes. The ground gets wet and boggy and there is a sparse line of marker posts. When a drystone wall is reached, turn left to follow it, still on wet and boggy ground. Go through a gate on the right and walk down a moorland slope of grass, sedge and rushes. Walk roughly parallel to a drystone wall, over a hump and down to **God's Bridge**. ◀ Walk up a track and go through a gate where there was once a railway bridge. Pass a cottage and climb towards the busy **A66 road**. This is too fast and dangerous to cross, so turn left until a concrete underpass is reached, then double back on the other side to reach the house called **Pasture End**.

This is a remarkable natural feature – a huge flat slab of actual limestone bedrock, with the River Greta flowing beneath it!

Climb a rushy slope, following a drystone wall to a corner. Walk straight ahead then drift to the right, later drifting to the left, while crossing **Rove Gill** on an undulating moor covered in patchy, varied vegetation. The moorland becomes heathery and the path is worn down to black peat. A series of cairns are passed, but one of them is actually the ruins of a small hut called **Ravock Castle**. Drift right and left on the way down to a track, hut, footbridge and gate, crossing **Deepdale Beck**.

Follow a drystone wall up a slope of grass, sedge and moss. Go over a slight rise and through a gate in a fence. Follow the wall across a boggy depression and climb further uphill, reaching the crest of **Race Yate** at 427m (1401ft). Desolate moorland stretches in all directions, and while this can be a fine place to walk in good weather, it can be a treadmill in foul weather. Walk downhill to pass through a gate where a fence joins a corner on the wall.

Walk straight ahead, gently down the moorland slope as signposted for the Pennine Way. Cross a boggy dip, then walk over a broad crest. The moorland is covered in tussocky grass and the path is rather vague. Watch carefully for a couple of helpful marker posts, as it is easy to be drawn off-course, especially in mist. A minor road is reached at a Pennine Way signpost. Turn left, walking down and then up a road to reach **Clove Lodge**, a farmhouse B&B. ▸

Strong walkers might consider pressing onwards to Middleton-in-Teesdale.

Alternative route

From **Trough Heads**, keep straight ahead alongside a drystone wall, as signposted 'Bowes Loop', along the edge of a rushy, mossy moor. When the wall turns left, turn with it and walk down to a corner. Go through a gate, through a field, through another gate and follow a gritty path to a farm road. Turn right to follow the road across a cattle grid and through fields, then keep left of the farm buildings at **East Mellwaters** to reach an access road.

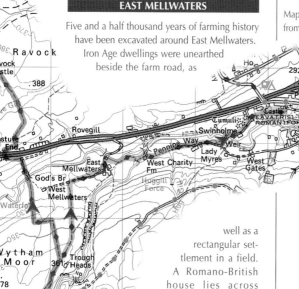

EAST MELLWATERS

Five and a half thousand years of farming history have been excavated around East Mellwaters. Iron Age dwellings were unearthed beside the farm road, as

Map continued from page 115

well as a rectangular settlement in a field. A Romano-British house lies across Sleightholme Beck, while the modern farmhouse stands on the site of a medieval dwelling. The farm provides specialist accommodation for people with disabilities, and a network of easy-use trails has been established around nearby fields – the Pennine Way uses some of them.

Walk towards the farmhouse, but turn left through a gate beside a barn, where the wall bears a signpost for the Pennine Way. Walk through a field, following the wall straight ahead, then turn left and go through the third gate in the wall. Follow a gritty path downstream and cross a footbridge. Keep left of the buildings ahead to reach an access track. Turn right through a gate and keep left of **West Charity Farm**, then turn left to follow the track through a couple of fields to the next farm, **Lady Myres**.

Follow the farm access road onwards and watch for a signpost pointing down through a gate in a wall below the road. Walk through a field and cross a footbridge above a weir on the **River Greta**. Walk downstream, but veer left, uphill and away from the river. Pass a farmhouse and continue along its access road. Turn right as indicated by a Pennine Way signpost, crossing a field and a stream to reach a step-stile to the right of a gate in a wall. Line up a series of stiles to pass through fields, keeping right of Bowes Castle. Turn left to follow a lane between the castle and St Giles' Church to enter **Bowes**.

BOWES

Travellers have crossed Stainmore for thousands of years, as this broad gap on the moors allows an obvious east–west link. The Romans regulated traffic by constructing a road equipped with forts, camps and signal stations. The fort at Bowes was called Lavatris, and its square, grassy platform can be discerned, but all its masonry was incorporated into Bowes Castle in 1170. The castle watched over an area that was an unsettled borderland. The Stainmore wastes were bleak, and monastic hospices were established to serve travellers. Memory of these places lingers in the place name

'spital'. A turnpike road was constructed in 1743 and literally paved the way for cross-country coaching. The South Durham and Lancashire Union railway came in 1861, lasting for a century until closure.

Facilities in Bowes include the Ancient Unicorn, a coaching inn around a courtyard that once provided stabling for horses and now provides food, drink and accommodation. There is a small post office/village shop, as well as a campsite. Bowes Castle can be visited free of charge at any time.

The 12th century Bowes Castle was built of stone taken from an earlier Roman fort

DAY 11

Baldersdale or Bowes to Middleton-in-Teesdale

Start	Clove Lodge, Baldersdale, NY 935 177
Alternative start	St Giles' Church, Bowes, NY 993 135
Finish	Middleton-in-Teesdale, NY 947 254
Distance	11km (7 miles); alternative 20km (12½ miles)
Ascent	300m (985ft); alternative 490m (1610ft)
Descent	400m (1310ft); alternative 540m (1770ft)
Maps	OS Landranger 91, OS Explorer OL31, Harvey's Pennine Way Central
Terrain	After an initial road-walk, gently rolling moorland with some wet and boggy patches. Also some fiddly field paths in the dales.
Refreshments	None until Middleton, then plenty of choice.

Walkers on the Bowes Loop alternative route spend all morning heading back to the Pennine Way main route in Baldersdale. First, the rolling moorlands of Stainmore are crossed, where the gritstone cap of Goldsborough is a prominent landmark. The Pennine Way through Baldersdale and Lunedale features a succession of reservoirs, and between them are the flowery hayfields of Hannah's Meadow nature reserve. Middleton-in-Teesdale lies a little off-route, but most walkers will visit the town, which is full of charm and interest. Those starting from Clove Lodge may wish to continue straight onwards to Langdon Beck.

Alternative route

Start at St Giles' Church in **Bowes** and follow the road west to the aptly named West End of the village, passing Dotheboys Hall. Turn right to cross a bridge over the busy **A66 road** and follow the road uphill, keeping left at a junction. The road is fenced and passes fields flanked by 'danger' signs. The former RAF Bowes Moor site on **Tute Hill** was used for the storage and disposal of chemical weapons. All that remains are a few ruins on a rushy moor, occasionally tested for lingering toxicity.

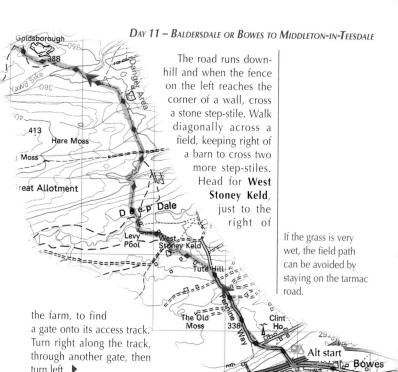

The road runs downhill and when the fence on the left reaches the corner of a wall, cross a stone step-stile. Walk diagonally across a field, keeping right of a barn to cross two more step-stiles. Head for **West Stoney Keld**, just to the right of

the farm, to find a gate onto its access track. Turn right along the track, through another gate, then turn left. ▶

If the grass is very wet, the field path can be avoided by staying on the tarmac road.

Follow a track straight ahead, over a cattle grid and down towards restored buildings at **Levy Pool**. Keep just to the left of these to find a footbridge over **Deepdale Beck**. Head downstream a little, then left uphill to follow a path indicated by marker posts. These lead over a grassy, rushy moor with some boggy patches. Cross a crest which offers good views of desolate, rolling Stainmore, then go down to cross a stream. Walk uphill and turn right along a firm path through bracken to reach a fence and a gate around 360m (1180ft). In very clear weather distant views stretch eastwards to the North York Moors and the smoky industrial Teesmouth.

Turn left to follow the fence, which leads to a wall and a roller-coaster walk over the moors. The wall has

Map continued on page 124

121

Abseiling on the distinctive gritstone outcrop of Goldsborough

been rebuilt, except for one old stretch where a stream flows through a gap. The wall gives way to a fence, which is also the boundary of a military firing range, marked by 'danger' signs. When the fence reaches a wall, there are two gates. Be sure to go through the one on the left, as the one on the right leads onto the firing range.

An extensive grass, rush and sedge moor stretches towards a hill with a distinctive gritstone cap. If the day is misty, then you will have to rely on following a vague path towards it, but in clear weather there is no problem. There is a slight dip in the moor, drained by the stream of **Yawd Sike**. Either ford it, or use a footbridge a little further upstream. The path keeps to the left of **Goldsborough**, whose gritstone crags form dramatic overhangs.

As a moorland crest is crossed around 370m (1215ft), Mickle Fell rises in the far distance while Baldersdale, closer to hand, is filled with three reservoirs. Keep left at path junctions to avoid descending too soon to a minor road. The road is eventually reached at a Pennine Way signpost. Turn left, then turn right down the access track to the farm of East Friar.

Squeeze past the building on the left and cross a stone step-stile on the left. A path heads straight across five fields, so line up stone step-stiles to pass from one to another. Drop down through another field to cross a bridge over a stream then climb to cross another stone step-stile. Head diagonally right, slightly downhill through a field to cross another stone step-stile, then head down to a three-way signpost where the Bowes Loop rejoins the main Pennine Way below **Clove Lodge**.

Main route

Leaving **Clove Lodge**, simply follow a track away from the farm, down through fields, passing the three-way signpost where the Bowes Loop rejoins the main route. Follow the track onwards, down through a stout iron gate, to cross Blackton Bridge at the head of **Blackton Reservoir**. A grassy track runs beside the reservoir, rising to a notice explaining about the Blackton nature reserve, which covers the head of the reservoir. Go through another stout iron gate to reach **Low Birk Hatt**, and turn left to follow the access road away from it, up through Hannah's Meadow nature reserve.

HANNAH'S MEADOW

Two flowery meadows beside the road are fine examples of North Pennine hayfields. Hannah Hauxwell, who achieved fame after being 'discovered' by a TV producer who was walking the Pennine Way, once managed these fields in a traditional manner, so that they are species-rich. She lived at Low Birk Hatt, and at the top of the fields, near High Birk Hatt, a barn can be visited by making a short detour along a duckboard path. The barn serves as a simple visitor centre for the reserve and also offers shelter in nasty weather.

Map continued on page 125

The road up through Hannah's Meadow reaches a gate and a minor road. Turn left, then right over a stone step-stile. Walk up a rushy, grassy slope and cross a little stream in a dip. Follow a wall uphill and cross the crest of **Hazelgarth Rigg** at 375m (1230ft), where there is a view of Lunedale ahead. Walk downhill and cross another little stream, eventually reaching a junction of walls. Cross a stone step-stile and follow a fence to another stone step-stile. Cross over and turn left downhill, but drift away from the wall to aim for a couple of

barns built beside each other in a field.
Cross two stone step-stiles to reach
them then keep right to pick up a
field path. Walk through three fields
using gates, reaching a road and
farm at **How**.

Turn right along the road,
then left as signposted for
the Pennine Way to
pass the

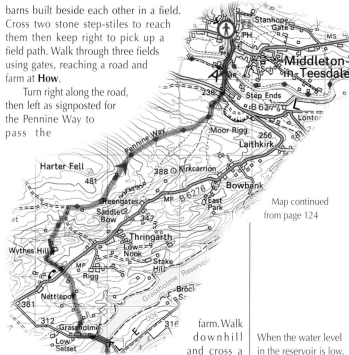

Map continued
from page 124

farm. Walk
downhill
and cross a
step-stile over a
fence to continue down through a wooded enclosure.
Turn right to cross two stone step-stiles to reach a road,
then turn left down the road to cross a five-arched stone
bridge over **Grassholme Reservoir**. ▸

When the water level
in the reservoir is low,
an older twin-arched
stone bridge is seen,
spanning the River
Lune and surrounded
by mudflats.

There is a picnic site to the right of the road, otherwise walk up the road to the farm of **Grassholme** and turn
right through the farmyard.

Walk down a stony track in a field then turn left up
a path as marked. The path is fairly straight, but if help is
needed to find stiles and gateways, then keep well left of
one barn on a crest, well right of another, before going
down into a dip, then well left of a third, on a crest, then
finally well left of a ruined barn beyond a dip. Walk up

125

The knoll of Kirkcarrion bears a distinctive plantation that makes it a local landmark

to the **B6276 road** and cross over it to follow a tarmac access road up to **Wythes Hill Farm**.

Keep left of the farm and left of a nearby house, following a track which later turns right down to a stream. Ford this and go through a gate, then climb towards the top corner of a field. Cross a stone step-stile and head diagonally up the next field, across a dip to cross a little stream, then up to a gap in a wall. Walk up the next field to join a track as it passes through a gate. Turn right to follow the track, and follow it from field to field, either using gates or stone step-stiles. Pass to the left of a ruined barn, and later keep to the right of a small building on the slopes of **Harter Fell**.

Go through a gate on a crest around 430m (1410ft). Middleton-in-Teesdale can be seen below, with a distinctive clump of trees on the knoll of Kirkcarrion away to the right. Walk down through a grassy field and go through a gate. A path runs down a broad, grassy slope with large patches of bracken and occasional rashes of boulders. Walk downhill and go through a gate in a fence. Further downhill, don't worry about a fork in the track, or a tangle of loops, since everything leads to a gate in a wall.

Walk straight downhill and cross an old railway trackbed, then go down a short, steep slope to reach a gate and a minor road. Turn right along the road, then left down the **B6276 road**. A campsite is signposted to the right, while the Pennine Way is later signposted to the left, beside a cattle mart. Most walkers will want to cross the bridge over the River Tees to detour into **Middleton-in-Teesdale**.

Middleton-in-Teesdale lies just off route, but most Pennine Wayfarers will visit the town

127

MIDDLETON-IN-TEESDALE

Middleton has a full range of facilities, including a hotel, B&Bs and a campsite. There is a bank with an ATM, a post office, cafés, shops and fish and chips. The only pub in town is owned by the local community. Regular daily buses run to Barnard Castle and Darlington. A minibus runs to Langdon Beck, except Sundays. A tourist information centre is also available (tel: 01833 641001).

Middleton has 12th-century origins and was close to the hunting and grazing grounds of distant Rievaulx Abbey. The Horsemarket and Market Place point to the settlement's importance in a farming region, and the old market cross and remains of the village stocks survive. Water from Hudeshope Beck powered two corn mills. St Mary's church dates from 1857, but an old arch and detached belfry belong to an earlier church dating from 1557. The churchyard holds the grave of Richard Watson, the celebrated miner-poet of Teesdale. Middleton became an important lead-mining centre and the town was developed by the London Lead Company.

THE LONDON LEAD COMPANY

The London Lead Company, or 'Quaker Company', after the religious persuasion of its directors, dominated mining activities in Teesdale and far beyond. The region was formerly the world's greatest producer of lead, and the company provided a stable continuity of employment and development for two centuries, from the 1700s to the 1900s. The company superintendant lived in grand style at Middleton House, while loyal employees could expect good accommodation and access to education and other services. At one time 90 per cent of Middleton's working population were employed directly by the company.

DAY 12
Middleton-in-Teesdale to Langdon Beck

Start	Middleton-in-Teesdale, NY 947 254
Finish	Langdon Beck Youth Hostel, NY 860 305
Distance	14km (8½ miles)
Ascent	230m (755ft)
Descent	80m (260ft)
Maps	OS Landranger 91, OS Explorer OL31, Harvey's Pennine Way Central
Terrain	Easy field paths and riverside paths, passing stunning waterfalls. The route drifts onto more rugged ground later then returns to the riverside.
Refreshments	Café off-route at Bowlees. Pub off-route at Langdon Beck.

This is a gentle and easy day's walk, and of course the temptation would be to extend it. It could be tagged onto the previous day's walk, or the following day's walk, but this should be resisted, partly in order to conserve energy for a couple of hard days ahead, but also because there is a lot to see and admire in Teesdale. Enjoy the gentle paths beside the River Tees and maybe detour to the Bowlees Visitor Centre to find out more about the natural wonders of Upper Teesdale. Spend time admiring spectacular waterfalls and look out for a range of wild flowers.

Bowlees lies just off the Pennine Way from Wynch Bridge, offering a visitor centre and a café

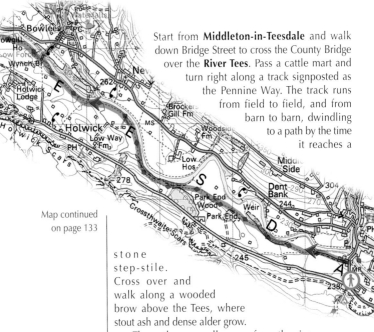

Start from **Middleton-in-Teesdale** and walk down Bridge Street to cross the County Bridge over the **River Tees**. Pass a cattle mart and turn right along a track signposted as the Pennine Way. The track runs from field to field, and from barn to barn, dwindling to a path by the time it reaches a

Map continued
on page 133

stone step-stile. Cross over and walk along a wooded brow above the Tees, where stout ash and dense alder grow.

The path soon pulls away from the river, avoiding sweeping meanders to take a direct line through flowery fields and grassy pastures, passing more trees and small woods. Cross stone step-stiles over drystone walls, as well as an iron ladder stile. Continue through fields with no views of the river. Climb a little and cross a stream at **Park End Wood** before catching sight of the Tees. Don't go up to a barn, but watch for a stone step-stile to continue parallel to the river. Notice how many farms and houses are painted white.

WHITEWASH

Dozens of whitewashed farmsteads are dotted throughout Teesdale, standing in stark contrast to the green fields. There are many tales to explain the colour scheme. One relates that the Duke of Cleveland was wandering lost on the moors in foul weather. He approached a house for shelter, believing it was occupied by his tenants, and was embarrassed to discover that it wasn't. He ordered all the buildings on his estate to be whitewashed, so that he wouldn't make the same mistake again! To this day, Raby Estate properties continue to be whitewashed, with their doorposts and lintels painted black. This doesn't apply south of the Tees, which is part of the Strathmore Estate.

Walk along a wooded brow then head down to cross a footbridge over a stream. Follow a path beside the bouldery, cobbly, swift and noisy **River Tees**. Pass a campsite and later reach a footbridge, Scoberry Bridge. Don't cross, but notice how a path leaves the footbridge and heads through fields on the left, leading up to the nearby village of **Holwick**.

HOLWICK

Holwick was once the most northerly village in Yorkshire, before being annexed to County Durham. From the River Tees, there is a glimpse of Holwick Lodge, which was built in the late 19th century. It looks palatial and is said to have been used by the late Queen Mother on her honeymoon. Other buildings in the village lie along a road at the foot of rugged cliffs on the Whin Sill. The Strathmore Arms offers food, drink, accommodation and camping. Low Way Farm offers food and drink at the Farmhouse Kitchen, as well as a bunkhouse and camping.

Further along the riverside path, pass a small waterfall where the Tees is constricted in a rocky channel. Lush greenery flanks a paved stretch of path as the Pennine Way enters the Upper Teesdale National Nature Reserve. When the Tees is seen beyond, it sports low falls and rapids, followed by a stretch where the river slides through a rocky channel with barely a ripple. Wynch Bridge and Low Force are soon reached among mixed woodland.

Low Force is a splendid waterfall, crashing twice over the hard rocky lip of the Whin Sill

WYNCH BRIDGE

In 1741 the first chain suspension bridge in the country was strung across the Tees. It collapsed in 1802 and was subsequently repaired and strengthened. The present bridge dates from 1830 and spans the rocky gorge close to the original site. It too has been strengthened and is only designed to allow one person to cross at a time. Crossing the bridge allows a detour off the Pennine Way to visit the nearby village of Bowlees.

BOWLEES VISITOR CENTRE

Pride of place in Bowlees is an old Methodist chapel converted into a fine visitor centre, operated by the Durham Wildlife Trust. The centre, which can be visited free, offers background information and displays relating to the geology, history and natural history of Teesdale. There are plenty of notes about wild flowers, and some species grow outside the building. There is helpful literature on sale, including plant guides specifically about the flowers of Upper Teesdale. There is also a small café on site (tel: 01833 622292).

Beyond Wynch Bridge, pass a stone sculpture of a couple of sheep, then pause to admire **Low Force**, where the Tees pours over a rock-step, then splits into two separate falls over another rock-step. A gravel path continues through a gate, passing riverside trees such as alder, birch and rowan. The path becomes rockier and the Tees alongside seems short of water. In fact, the river splits around a large island and only a little water is seen below. An easy grass or gravel path leads onwards beside the main flow, reaching a footbridge, Holwick Head Bridge. Don't cross, unless intending to visit the High Force Hotel on the other side of the river.

Crazy paving and steps lead up a slope of flowery turf where delightful little mountain pansies grow. Walk through a gate to follow a gravel path, with birch to the right and juniper to the left. Soon, the land either side of the path is covered in juniper and bracken – this is the most extensive juniper wood in the country. There is no sight of the Tees, but a rumbling sound gives away the location of **High Force**.

Map continued from page 130

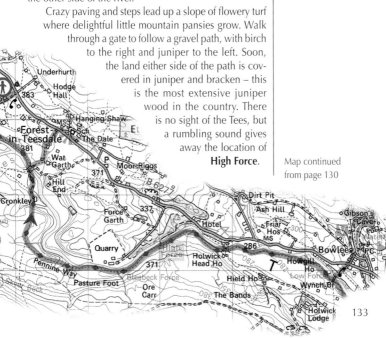

High Force is England's most powerful waterfall and sometimes the whole cliff face is covered in water

HIGH FORCE

The best view of England's most powerful waterfall is from a spur path on the right, before reaching the fall, leading to a cliff-top perch. Don't miss it, or the only other view is from the top of the fall. Enjoy the spectacle of water pouring furiously from a rocky channel, over a rock-step, boiling in a turbulent pool, before rushing through a deep and rocky gorge. This is all seen for free, while people in the gorge have paid for access from the High Force Hotel.

Go through a kissing gate at the top of the waterfall and continue upstream along a gravel path. This becomes rough and bouldery among bracken and heather later. Cross a footbridge below the little waterfall of **Bleabeck Force**. Walk along an easy path where rapid progress can be made at **Pasture Foot**, which is welcome, since there is a noisy, dusty quarry cutting into the Whin Sill on the opposite side of the river.

THE WHIN SILL

Many dramatic landforms in Upper Teesdale, around the North Pennines and into Northumberland owe their existence to the Whin Sill. This enormous sheet of dolerite was forced into the limestone bedrock under immense pressure in a molten state around 295 million years ago. As the heat dissipated, the limestone in contact with the dolerite baked until its structure altered, forming peculiar 'sugar limestone', which breaks down into a soil preferred by many of Teesdale's wild flowers.

While weathering, the Whin Sill proves more resistant than the rocks above and below it, so it forms dramatic landforms such as Holwick Scars, Cronkley Scar and Falcon Clints. Where the Whin Sill occurs in the bed of the Tees, its abrupt step creates splendid waterfalls such as Low Force, High Force, Bleabeck Force and Cauldron Snout. Later on the Pennine Way, it is responsible for the cliffs of High Cup and the rugged crest bearing Hadrian's Wall. The Whin Sill has been quarried throughout Teesdale, generally being crushed and used as a durable road-stone.

Cross two footbridges close together at **Skyer Beck**, then the path weaves between fenced-off areas of juniper, where regeneration involves controlling grazing. Walk up stone-slab and duckboard steps on a wet slope. Continue up a firm slope of close-cropped green turf studded with boulders. On top of a grassy crest, a stone bears two arrows. Left is 'GT', for the Green Trod over Cronkley Fell. Right is 'PW' for the Pennine Way. The path is paved with flagstones, heading down into a dip and crossing a stile over a fence.

Follow a wall uphill and go through a gate in a fence. The flagstone path crosses a wet and rushy area, then walk downhill beside the wall. Go through a little gated stile on the right then continue down through a breach in the Whin Sill, where the path is rugged underfoot and juniper covers nearby slopes. Walk up a path to reach the farm of **Cronkley**. Go through the farmyard and walk

Many species thrive here simply because the ground is unstable, preventing other species from colonising the slope and crowding out the rarities.

down the access track, passing flowery meadows before crossing a bridge over the **River Tees**.

Turn left to follow the Pennine Way upstream. A narrow path beside the river passes through a kissing gate and crosses a slope of boulder clay subject to slow landslip. Rather than curse the uneven cobbles and mud, spend a while admiring the impressive array of wild flowers. ◄ The path passes the confluence of the River Tees and Langdon Beck, and the latter is followed upstream.

The lonely looking farm of **Wheysike House** is seen across the broad and bouldery river. The riverside path is rather narrow as it runs beside a wall, and it seems doomed to collapse into the river and require diverting soon. When Saur Hill Bridge is reached, the Pennine Way turns left to cross it. However, anyone stopping for the night at **Langdon Beck** will need to head off-route.

Langdon Beck is a sizeable river, with the remote Wheysike House standing on the opposite bank

LANGDON BECK

Facilities are limited around Langdon Beck and Forest-in-Teesdale, and it is not obvious where to find everything. Two farmhouse B&Bs are located close to the school in Forest-in-Teesdale and one of them offers a basic campsite. Both can be approached by leaving the Pennine Way at Cronkley Bridge, following a field path directly up to the B6272 road. Langdon Beck Youth Hostel is best approached from Saur Hill Bridge a little further on. Don't cross the bridge, but follow the farm access track up to the B6272 road and turn left to reach the hostel. For the Langdon Beck Hotel, however, cross Saur Hill Bridge and turn right to continue upstream to the next road. Turn right to walk to the hotel at a junction with the B6277 road.

DAY 13
Langdon Beck to Dufton

Start	Langdon Beck Youth Hostel, NY 860 305
Finish	Stag Inn, Dufton, NY 689 251
Distance	22km (13½ miles)
Ascent	330m (1085ft)
Descent	530m (1740ft)
Maps	OS Landranger 91, OS Explorer OL19, Harvey's Pennine Way Central
Terrain	Riverside paths give way to moorland paths. The ascent is gradual, while the descent is rugged at first, with a steep track and road at the end.
Refreshments	Pub at Dufton.

This is a wonderfully varied day, starting in the flowery meadows and hay-fields of Upper Teesdale, over 350m (1150ft). The Pennine Way follows the River Tees upstream to the powerful Cauldron Snout. There are fine little falls on Maize Beck during a moorland traverse in the middle of the day. A footbridge installed in recent years avoids the need to use a former 'flood route'. High Cup appears suddenly and boasts a stunning symmetry, where the Whin Sill forms cliffs on either side of the valley. A long descent leads to the charming village of Dufton, built of red sandstone on the fringe of the Vale of Eden.

Start from **Langdon Beck Youth Hostel**, turn left along the road, then right down a farm access road to cross a bridge over **Langdon Beck**. The Pennine Way turns left just before the farm at Saur Hill. Cross a grassy rise to find the first of a few white-painted stone step-stiles. Walk from one to another through fields that have occasional short duckboards over wet patches. The path runs along a brow overlooking the **River Tees** then gradually drops down to run alongside it. Stay close to the river, keeping away from **Widdybank Farm**.

At Cauldron Snout, the River Tees cascades furiously down a channel cut into the Whin Sill

Map continued on page 140

WIDDYBANK FARM

Haymaking comes late around Widdybank Farm compared to farms further down Teesdale, owing to the altitude and resulting lower temperatures. Flowers growing in this area have a chance to ripen and drop their seeds before mowing takes place, resulting in

Progress is slow as the Pennine Way grapples with boulder scree around Falcon Clints

self-regenerating, species-rich meadows. The farm is a base for Natural England staff working on the Upper Teesdale and Moor House National Nature Reserves.

Join and follow a track away from the farm, through a gate and further upstream at **Holmwath**. The track becomes a broad carpet of short green grass. After passing through a kissing gate, the riverside path crosses small boulders, a duckboard, then big, awkward boulders. Alternating duckboard and paved stretches pass a juniper-covered island in the Tees. The path becomes rough and bouldery again, with crumbling, baked rock revealed beneath the whinstone cliffs of **Falcon Clints**, with an impressive amount of wild thyme.

Map continued on page 142

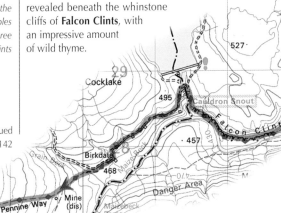

Cross some big, awkward boulders, then follow easy stretches of flagstone path and duckboards, keeping walkers off a boulder-scree and bog. More wild thyme grows on the dry parts, while bog asphodel grows on the wet parts. After one last stretch of boulder-hopping, the path reaches the confluence of the River Tees and Maize Beck, for a sudden view of **Cauldron Snout**.

The Tees is confined to a steep and narrow rock gorge, where the water boils furiously as it beats against the walls and tumbles over rock-steps. You will need to use your hands to scramble up big, chunky rock-steps alongside. The rock can be slippery when wet, and has been polished by the boots of previous visitors. At the top of the falls, a flagstone path leads to a narrow road beneath the concrete dam of **Cow Green Reservoir**.

COW GREEN RESERVOIR

Cow Green Reservoir was constructed to slake the thirst of Teesmouth and its burgeoning industries. Sadly, an area rich in rare plants was drowned, despite vociferous protests, though some last-minute transplantation took place. The dam was built between 1967 and 1970 and holds 41 million cubic metres of water (9000 million gallons). The surface of the water covers 310 hectares (770 acres) and is 489m (1603ft) above sea level. Water is not piped away, but merely impounded and released as required, so that the flow of the River Tees can be regulated, allowing water to be abstracted far downstream at Broken Scar, for domestic use, and at Blackwell and Yarm, for industrial use.

Turn left to follow the road over a bridge, then keep left to follow a track over a cattle grid to cross a rushy rise near a barn. The track undulates onwards, crossing another cattle grid and passing a couple more barns, before reaching a remote farm at **Birkdale**. Pass in front of the farmhouse and follow the track through a couple of fields to reach **Grain Beck**, to cross a footbridge. Ahead lie extensive, open and exposed moorlands.

A flagstone path climbs easily up a grassy, rushy moorland and a stony track winds further uphill, eventually climbing onto an old mine spoil at Moss Shop. Nearby is a flagpole that will usually be flying a red flag. ◄ A black peat path beyond the mine spoil quickly gives way to a firm stony path. The moorland is heather and grass, mossy in places, with sedge, rushes and a little bog cotton. The stony path later gives way to a flagstone path. Further along, the flagstones give way to a grassy path over blanket bog that can be squelchy underfoot. A couple of drainage ditches are bridged then all of a sudden, a firm path is reached where the bedrock is limestone. The ground rises to around 590m (1935ft) on **Rasp Hill**, speckled with flowers and abundant thistles. Rising on the skyline are some of the bleakest, boggiest and most forbidding moorlands in England, such as Mickle Fell, Little Fell, Murton Fell and Meldon Hill.

The undulating path heads gradually downhill, and a marker post with an arrow helps to define it where a quad-bike track crosses over it. Blanket bog again features grass, sedge and rushes, with little bridges across drainage ditches, and several wet patches. Further downhill there is a stretch of flagstone path, then firmer ground is reached as the path drops towards **Maize Beck**. Head upstream along a pleasant strip of limestone grassland, passing a spring near an attractive little waterfall over a rock-step.

This marks the boundary of a military firing range, the Warcop Training Area. At no point does the Pennine Way enter it, but 'danger' notices are seen at regular intervals.

Map continued on page 144

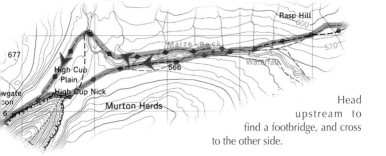

Head upstream to find a footbridge, and cross to the other side.

Walk along a short flagstone path and turn right to continue upstream, though gradually climbing above the beck. The path is covered in uneven stones and crosses a grassy, rushy slope. The path becomes easier once it is routed along another band of limestone, where the path is smooth and covered in short, green turf. The path climbs gently uphill, pulls away from the beck and crosses the broad and level gap of **High Cup Plain**.

Watch for occasional upright stone slabs beside the path, especially in mist, as one of them bears a carved arrow indicating a right turn downhill. The path quickly reaches a little stream that passes through a rocky cleft at **High Cup Nick**. Cross the stream and walk on the level rocky top of the Whin Sill, and be sure to seek out great viewpoints to appreciate the striking lines of columnar cliffs on either side of **High Cup**. In the distance, the eastern parts of the Lake District can be seen across the Vale of Eden. Climb uphill a little and follow a path along a limestone terrace along the northern rim of the valley. Walk on pleasant short turf, with the whinstone cliffs below and boulder-scree above. ▶

Watch carefully for a brief glimpse of Nichol's Chair – a whinstone pinnacle. According to a local story, Nichol was a Dufton cobbler who scaled the column, then soled and heeled a pair of shoes on top.

The Pennine Way originally stayed close to the edge along a natural paved path called **Narrowgate**, but has

High Cup Nick is a rocky cleft at the head of High Cup, cut into the cliffs of the Whin Sill

143

been diverted a little further uphill onto a roller-coaster path crossing boulder-scree and flagstones. Either way, the route crosses a couple of gushing streams then there is a single path marked later. Leaving High Cup, the path rises and falls across slopes of grass, sedge and rushes, with views of the whole of the Lake District and the northern parts of the Yorkshire Dales. It can be rough and stony where the bedrock is sandstone, or smooth where the bedrock is limestone. One stretch runs down a slope of sandstone boulders, while later the track winds down a limestone edge at **Peeping Hill** to reach a drystone wall and gates.

Cross a step-stile beside a gate and walk through a sheepfold to pick up a stony track leading down a steep and grassy slope. The track swings right and aims directly towards the conical form of Dufton Pike, passing through a gate. It later swings left, more directly downhill, passing through another gate. Now enclosed by drystone walls, the track passes a number of large trees, the first seen since Birkdale, then it continues as a narrow road passing **Bow Hall**.

The road passes large, rough pastures, and there are a lot of gorse bushes along one stretch. When a road junction is reached, turn right uphill to enter the village of **Dufton**, and follow the road to Dufton Hall. Note that the Pennine Way turns right here, but anyone heading for the central village green should turn left and right by road, returning to Dufton Hall to pick up the route again. The Stag Inn is located in the centre of the village.

Map continued
from page 142

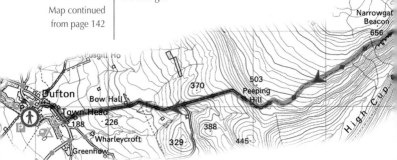

Nichol's Chair is reputed to have been climbed by a cobbler from Dufton

DUFTON

The village is an Anglo-Saxon settlement, originally formed of simple huts arranged around a broad green. This allowed animals to be corralled, and in later times safeguarded them from border reivers and raiders. In the early 17th century the houses were rebuilt in red sandstone, then further improvements came in the 18th century with the support of the London Lead Company, or 'Quaker Company'. Lead was mined in Great Rundale, ceasing around 1900, but barytes was mined until 1924. More recently the spoil has been worked for fluorspar, which was originally a 'waste' mineral.

Accommodation in Dufton is limited to a handful of B&Bs and a youth hostel, with a campsite also available. The Stag Inn offers food and drink and the hostel has a small food store. Most facilities lie around the central green, where towering lime trees grow. There is an attractive old water pump, installed by the London Lead Company. A very limited bus service links Dufton with Appleby, which has a full range of services, but lies 5km (3 miles) off-route.

The ornate drinking fountain on the green in Dufton was provided by the London Lead Company

DAY 14
Dufton to Alston

Start	Stag Inn, Dufton, NY 689 251
Finish	The Firs, Alston, NY 716 461
Distance	32km (20 miles)
Ascent	1040m (3410ft)
Descent	940m (3085ft)
Maps	OS Landranger 86 or 87 and 91, OS Explorer OL19 and OL31, Harvey's Pennine Way Central
Terrain	The highest, most remote and most exposed part of the route. Mostly good paths and tracks, but careful route-finding required on the initial ascent, and over Cross Fell, where paths are vague. Most of the descent is along a clear track.
Refreshments	Pub at Garrigill. Plenty of choice at Alston.

This is the longest and toughest day on the Pennine Way. It can be shortened by calling a halt at Garrigill, and in case of real difficulty, the route can be abandoned before Great Dun Fell, where there is a road, or beyond Cross Fell, where Greg's Hut offers basic shelter. In clear weather, this is a splendid stage, climbing high and staying high, enjoying wide-ranging views. However, these hills hold the English records for bad weather. Spare a thought for the miners who once had to live and work high on the moors, enduring cold, damp and the slow poisoning of their health in lead mines.

To leave **Dufton**, pick up the course of the Pennine Way from the corner of the road beside Dufton Hall, where the route is signposted along a track. Follow the track down into a dip, then turn left through a gate to follow a flagstone path enclosed by trees. This gives way to a fenced path between fields, passing through gates. Cross a stream and follow the path up past some trees. Continue straight along a track to pass a bungalow and **Coatsike Farm**. ▶

Go straight through the farmyard and follow a grassy track through gates. The way is quickly flanked by ash

A short-cut is available from Dufton. Take the road heading for Knock and turn right to follow the access track to Coatsike Farm.

The highest Pennine
summits are in view
ahead, with the
foothills of Dufton
Pike to the right and
Knock Pike to the left.
The Lake District is
behind, far across the
Vale of Eden. ◄

and hawthorn, and as the rugged track climbs it diminishes to a sunken path, passing a ruined farmhouse at Halsteads. Continue straight ahead, following a track over a grassy rise and down to a gate. Cross a stone 'clapper' footbridge over **Great Rundale Beck**, then walk up the track and turn right to climb straight uphill, alongside a wall, on a rushy slope. ◄

Go through a couple of gates and the track turns sharp left, away from the wall, climbing up a grassy, rushy moorland slope. When a signpost for the Pennine Way is reached, turn left along a narrow, grassy path. Cross a stone step-stile over a wall and walk across a slope of heather and bilberry. Cross another stone step-stile to reach a stout footbridge spanning **Swindale Beck**.

Climb a few stone steps and pass a sign announcing the Moor House and Upper Teesdale National Nature Reserves. Follow a narrow, grassy path up a steep, grassy slope bearing rashes of boulders. Throughout the climb, steep and gentle slopes

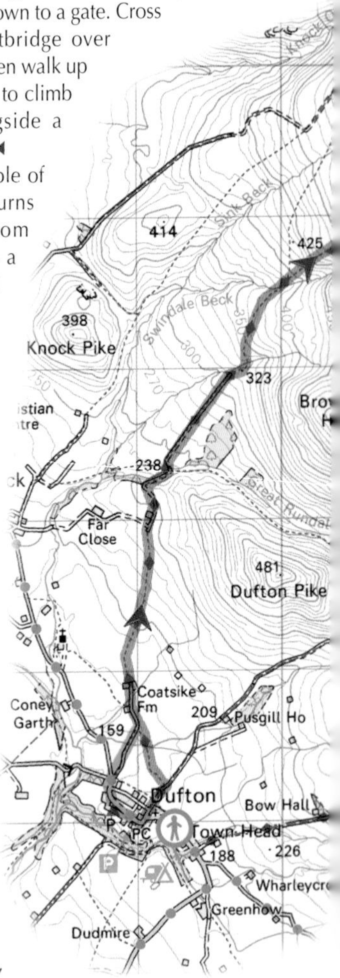

Map continued
on page 152

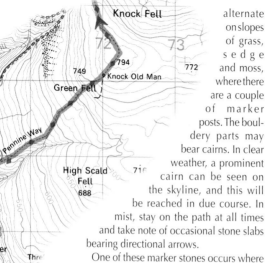

alternate on slopes of grass, sedge and moss, where there are a couple of marker posts. The boul-dery parts may bear cairns. In clear weather, a prominent cairn can be seen on the skyline, and this will be reached in due course. In mist, stay on the path at all times and take note of occasional stone slabs bearing directional arrows.

One of these marker stones occurs where the path swings left and climbs alongside a straight stream, known locally as a 'hush', formed by miners continually damming and releasing water to scour the hillside, exposing the bedrock in the hope of finding mineral veins. At the top of the hush, a small ruined hut can be seen away to the left. The path crosses a wet, peaty shelf, then more marker stones indicate a path winding up a steep limestone slope, which is firm and dry underfoot.

The path finally reaches a large, square-built cairn on a boulder-strewn moor. This is the cairn that was seen earlier on the skyline, called **Knock Old Man**. In mist, be aware that it does *not* mark the summit. Climb a little further at a gentle gradient to reach a final hump and a smaller cairn on **Knock Fell**, at 794m (2605ft). This is the highest point so far along the Pennine Way, but its moment of glory is short-lived and soon to be eclipsed!

Veer left to pick up the path leaving the summit, though the line gets lost among black peat and stony patches, grass and sedge. In clear weather, this is no problem since the 'radome' on the top of Great Dun Fell is a prominent feature to aim for, but in mist great care needs to be taken to locate a flagstone path downhill. This winds between bog pools and has a couple of gaps in its course. The flags run out as the path crosses firmer ground on a gap where the bedrock is limestone.

In foul weather, if you are inclined to abandon the route, turn left to follow the road down to the village of Knock and return to Dufton.

Step up onto a road and turn right to follow it gently uphill. ◀

There is a barrier across the road, as well as a gate across a track on the right. The Pennine Way simply leaves the road, avoids the track, and climbs straight uphill. Another 'hush' is encountered and the path climbs alongside, then turns right to cross it using a few steps. Climb to the 'radome' on top of **Great Dun Fell**, at 848m (2782ft). Once again, this is the highest point so far along the Pennine Way, and once again it will be surpassed!

GREAT DUN FELL

The big white 'radome' makes Great Dun Fell unmistake-able in distant views. National Air Traffic Services

Map continued on page 152

The endlessly rolling moorlands of the North Pennines as seen from Great Dun Fell

monitors aircraft as well as the weather. Among decades of weather archives lie some all-England records for weather stations, including the greatest number of foggy days, the highest wind speed and the most prolonged frost. Bear in mind that the annual mean temperature is only 4°C, while over 200 days may feature mist, and over 100 days feature gale-force winds! The road to the 'radome' is the highest in England. Note how lush the grass and flowers are inside the compound fence, compared to the bleak sheep-grazed moorlands stretching endlessly beyond.

Leaving the summit is no problem in clear weather, but in mist be sure to pick up the flagstone path that offers a sure guide north-west. The path crosses grass, sedge, moss and bog cotton, but shortly after rising from a gap the flagstones finish. Climb straight up a steep, grassy slope and walk along a broad crest of short turf, passing a cairn. The summit of **Little Dun Fell** is 842m (2762ft) and the crest becomes boulder-strewn, bearing a couple of shelter cairns.

Pass left of the cairns and follow a vague path down a boulder-studded grassy slope. A long flagstone path leads almost to a broad and boggy gap at **Tees Head**, where there is bog cotton and a National Nature Reserve notice. Follow a flagstone path up through a kissing gate in an

151

electric fence. The path has steps and climbs a rugged slope to pass a spring among masses of moss. Climb further up a bouldery slope to reach a tall cairn on a gentle, boulder-strewn slope. In mist, proceed with care as there is only a vaguely trodden path leading to another cairn, and it is necessary to walk across a broad plateau to reach the summit cairn, trig point and cross-shelter on **Cross Fell**, at 893m (2930ft).

CROSS FELL

This is the highest point on the Pennine Way and the highest point in England outside the Lake District. Imagine how high it would be if it rose to a peak, instead of being a flat plateau. It used to be called Fiends Fell, recorded as such in 1340 and 1479. William Camden, writing in *Britannica*, published in 1586, said that a cross had been planted on the summit to banish the 'fiends'. It

Map continued on page 156

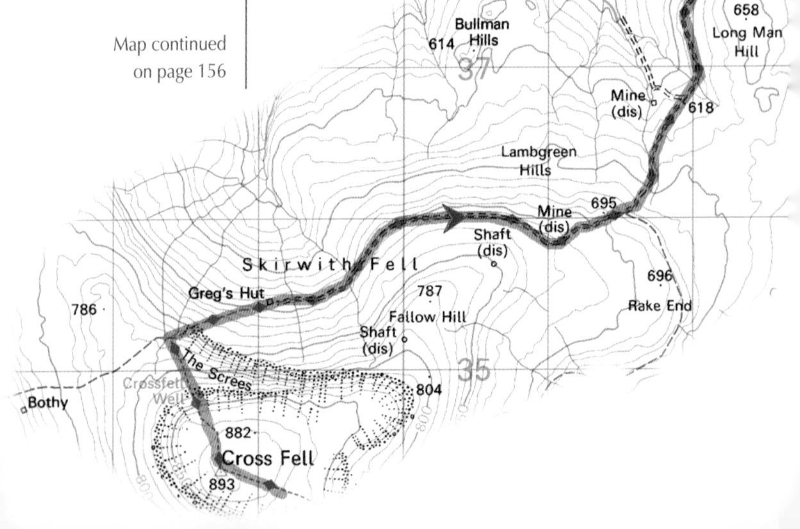

616

Pikeman Hill

658
Long Man Hill

Bullman Hills
614

Mine (dis)
618

Lambgreen Hills

Mine (dis)
695

Skirwith Fell

Greg's Hut

786

787

Fallow Hill

Shaft (dis)

696
Rake End

Shaft (dis)

The Screes

Crossfell Wells

804

Bothy

882
Cross Fell

893

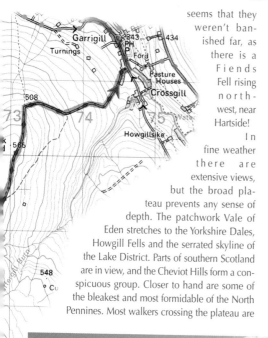

seems that they weren't banished far, as there is a Fiends Fell rising north-west, near Hartside!

In fine weather there are extensive views, but the broad plateau prevents any sense of depth. The patchwork Vale of Eden stretches to the Yorkshire Dales, Howgill Fells and the serrated skyline of the Lake District. Parts of southern Scotland are in view, and the Cheviot Hills form a conspicuous group. Closer to hand are some of the bleakest and most formidable of the North Pennines. Most walkers crossing the plateau are

View from Cross Fell to Little and Great Dun Fell, home of English records for extreme weather

aware of the dimpled ground underfoot. Look carefully and you will see that slight humps of stones are separated by lower areas of gravel. These are 'stone polygons', formed by repeated freezing and thawing of the ground since the Ice Age.

Leaving the summit of Cross Fell, a vague path is marked by cairns, and there are pieces of flagstones scattered around as the ground begins to fall. Expect lots of wet and boggy ground on the way downhill, where multiple paths try to outflank difficulties. A large cairn is reached where a clear path, known as the Corpse Road, slices across the hillside. Turn right to follow it downhill, passing sink holes and joining a track at **Greg's Hut**.

GREG'S HUT

This remote bothy was once a mining 'shop', or a lodging house for miners who lived and worked in this remote place, only going home at weekends. It stands at 700m (2300ft) and offers basic shelter to considerate users. In foul weather, bear in mind that only half the distance between Dufton and Garrigill has been covered, and the Pennine Way stays remarkably high on the moors for most of the way to Garrigill.

Greg's Hut, a former mine 'shop', now serves as a bothy at 700m (2300ft) on the slopes of Cross Fell

Leave **Greg's Hut** by walking along the track, gently downhill, then gradually uphill, passing a couple more ruins associated with old lead mines. There are views across Alston Moor and far beyond to the distant Cheviot Hills. When the track crosses a moorland rise above the **Lambgreen Hills**, there is a view back to Cross Fell, Little Dun Fell, Great Dun Fell, Knock Fell and the Cow Green Reservoir. The track winds down past old mine spoil, where little chips of purple fluorspar catch the eye. Keep straight ahead where another stony track heads off to the right to **Rake End**.

Walk down the winding track, through a gate, and continue with a fence running parallel on the right, though it later drifts away. Keep straight ahead at another junction, where a track heads off to the left, and again keep straight ahead where another track heads off to the right. A gradual climb leads across a rushy slope on **Long Man Hill**. The track undulates across the high moors on **Pikeman Hill**, at 616m (2021ft), where there is later grass and heather. A fence appears on the right and runs alongside the track. Go through a gate and cross another heather moor, where a drystone wall appears on the right.

Go through a gate and the track climbs gently with walls on both sides, still running across grass and heather moorland. The track is enclosed throughout its descent from the moors, turning a series of corners as it drops down past fields into South Tynedale. **Garrigill** is in view long before it is reached. Turn left along a road to reach the green in the middle of the village.

GARRIGILL

For many years this little village lacked accommodation, causing the vicar to throw open the doors of the church to offer shelter to Wayfarers descending late from Cross Fell. The George and Dragon Inn and post office shop look onto a fine green, but face an uncertain future. There are a small number of B&Bs available. An informal campsite is available behind the village hall.

Leave Garrigill along the road signposted for Leadgate. The road runs beside the **River South Tyne** then when it climbs above it, turn right to cross a stone step-stile beside a gate, and follow a track to some spoil heap and assorted junk. Bear left to pass this and cross a stile, then follow a path up a grassy bank to walk beside a stand of Scots pine. Walk down a grassy slope and follow a wooded riverside path that may be overgrown, crossing stiles to emerge in a field and reach a footbridge.

Cross the River South Tyne and turn left, following the path away from the river to reach a farmhouse at **Sillyhall**. Follow a field path as marked, over a rise to reach the farm of **Bleagate**. Turn left between the buildings and then right to continue through fields. The path stays away from the river, crossing stone step-stiles or passing through gaps in walls. Pass below a couple of houses and head down to cross a footbridge over a stream. The path continues through fields, then up onto a brow, passing between fields and big beech trees. This stretch is known as The Firs, reaching

Map continued
from page 152

the youth hostel at the bottom end of **Alston**. The Pennine Way is signposted left down a path, where steps lead to a road, but most Wayfarers will wish to enter the town, in which case they should keep straight ahead.

ALSTON

Alston claims to be the highest market town in England, It rises from the banks of the River South Tyne at 280m (920ft), reaching 320m (1050ft) at a primary school at the top of the town. The

Alston's Market Cross on Front Street has been demolished twice by runaway lorries!

Market Cross in the town centre is essentially a roof supported on stone pillars. It has been demolished by runaway trucks, not once, but twice. It was gifted to the town in 1765 by William Stephenson, an Alston man who became Mayor of London. St Augustine's Church is easily spotted because of its tall tower. Several fine stone buildings have been erected by public subscription. It is well worth wandering round quaint and poky back alleys, such as The Butts, once used for archery practice, and Gossipgate.

Most of Alston's facilities are arranged beside the steep, cobbled Front Street, where a shopping trip needs careful planning to avoid unnecessary ascents and descents! Alston has one of the best range of services on the Pennine Way. There are banks with ATMs, a post office, plenty of shops, including two fish and chip shops, as well as pubs and cafés. A range of accommodation includes hotels, B&Bs, a youth hostel and a campsite. Buses run daily, except Sundays, to Carlisle and Haltwhistle, with summer bus services to Penrith, Keswick, Hexham and Newcastle. The South Tyne Railway (**www.strps.co.uk**) runs a short distance from Alston to Kirkhaugh. A tourist information centre is also available (tel: 01434 382244).

DAY 15
Alston to Greenhead

Start	The Firs, Alston, NY 716 461
Finish	Greenhead Hotel, NY 660 654
Distance	27km (17 miles)
Ascent	540m (1770ft)
Descent	700m (2295ft)
Maps	OS Landranger 86, OS Explorer 31 and 43, Harvey's Pennine Way Central
Terrain	The route runs through a valley, but includes several ascents and descents, in and out of fields, using paths and tracks. Paths become vague as the route heads across broad and boggy moorlands.
Refreshments	Occasional buffet car at Kirkhaugh Station. Pub off-route at Knarsdale. Pub and tearoom at Greenhead.

On the map, this seems like an easy day's walk, but it can be time-consuming negotiating fiddly field paths. The Pennine Way wanders up and down the slopes of South Tynedale using vague paths, passing houses and farms, crossing stiles and going through gates. In recent years, the trackbed of the South Tyne Railway has been converted into the South Tyne Trail, which could be used to short-cut swiftly and easily from Alston to Knarsdale. The course of the Maiden Way Roman road is used to cross low moorlands. Later, there is awkward route-finding over Hartleyburn Common and Wain Rigg.

SOUTH TYNE RAILWAY

The Newcastle & Carlisle Railway Company originally planned a railway from Haltwhistle to the lead mines at Nenthead, but later decided to terminate the line at Alston, abandoning what would have been a steep climb onwards. The line was constructed between 1851 and 1852, featuring nine viaducts spanning the River South Tyne and some of its tributaries. As well as transporting

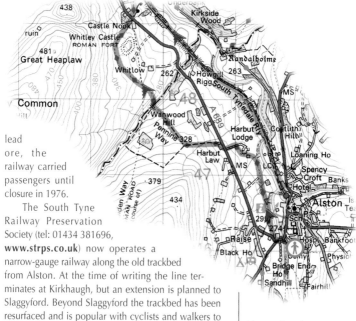

lead
ore, the
railway carried
passengers until
closure in 1976.

The South Tyne
Railway Preservation
Society (tel: 01434 381696,
www.strps.co.uk) now operates a
narrow-gauge railway along the old trackbed
from Alston. At the time of writing the line ter-
minates at Kirkhaugh, but an extension is planned to
Slaggyford. Beyond Slaggyford the trackbed has been
resurfaced and is popular with cyclists and walkers to
Haltwhistle.

Map continued
on page 160

Leave The Firs at **Alston** by walking down a short
flight of steps on a wooded slope to reach the main A686
road. Turn left to cross a bridge over the **River South Tyne**,
then turn right at a junction with the A689 signposted for
Brampton. Almost immediately, turn right down a track
and turn left to avoid a house. Walk through a wood and
up towards another house. Keep left to pass the house
using a narrow, enclosed path. Walk straight ahead along
a field path, passing an old gateway and crossing a wide,
grassy bridge over a stream. Turn left up towards **Harbut
Lodge**.

Keep left of all the buildings, then turn right and follow the edge of a field. Step over a wall and turn left up
a track to reach the A689 road. Turn right to pass **Harbut
Law**, which offers B&B, then turn left as signposted for
the Pennine Way. Pass through a couple of gates and
pass a barn, then follow a narrow, grassy path straight

159

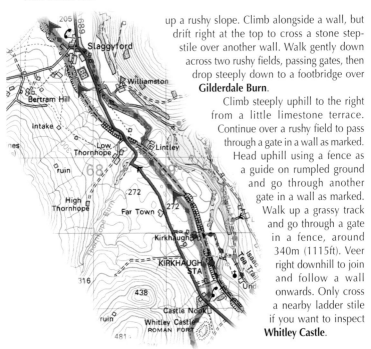

up a rushy slope. Climb alongside a wall, but drift right at the top to cross a stone step-stile over another wall. Walk gently down across two rushy fields, passing gates, then drop steeply down to a footbridge over **Gilderdale Burn**.

Climb steeply uphill to the right from a little limestone terrace. Continue over a rushy field to pass through a gate in a wall as marked. Head uphill using a fence as a guide on rumpled ground and go through another gate in a wall as marked. Walk up a grassy track and go through a gate in a fence, around 340m (1115ft). Veer right downhill to join and follow a wall onwards. Only cross a nearby ladder stile if you want to inspect **Whitley Castle**.

Map continued on page162

WHITLEY CASTLE

All that remains of this hillside Roman fort is the square ground plan and an impressive series of parallel embankments and ditches – up to eight of them at one point. Two corners stand proud, where watch-towers would have stood. The site affords fine views over South Tynedale and the fort was an important point on the Maiden Way Roman road, a stretch of which is followed later.

The wall leads to another ladder stile. Cross it and walk down towards the farm of **Castle Nook**. Don't enter the farmyard, but duck left into a woodland and cross a stream, then follow a path down to the A689 road. Cross over and go through a gate, then head left down towards

Refreshments are available at Kirkhaugh only when the train hauls a buffet car to the station

a building. Keep right of this and other houses, passing through gates. A field path runs gently down towards a farm, and the embankment of the South Tyne Railway is seen to the right. ▸

Turn left up a narrow farm access road at **Kirkhaugh**, then right as signposted for the Pennine Way just above the farm. Look ahead to spot ladder stiles to pass through a couple of fields then go through a gate in the next field. Don't head downhill, but contour across a slope to find another ladder stile. Two more ladder stiles need to be crossed before the field path runs along the foot of the old railway embankment. Cross over the access track serving the nearby farm of **Lintley**. Do not approach the farm, but cross a footbridge over **Thornhope Burn**, then turn right to pass under a railway viaduct.

A well-wooded riverside path, often overgrown later, leads to a small field where the broad and brown River South Tyne is followed downstream. The path crosses a steep, wooded slope then runs easily through another field. As the path broadens, it climbs to the A689 road, where a right turn leads straight to the village of **Slaggyford**. Turn left to follow a road up through the

There is access to Kirkhaugh Station, where a buffet car offers refreshments when trains arrive.

161

village green, then turn right at the Yew Tree Chapel B&B. A track leads gently uphill among trees, running parallel to the old railway trackbed. Don't join, cross or follow the trackbed, but follow the track uphill, until it diminishes to a path and runs downhill. Stout stone 'PW' markers keep walkers on course.

Cross a little footbridge and walk down into a wooded valley to cross a footbridge over **Knar Burn** below a towering stone viaduct. Turn right to reach a field, then left to find an arch under the old railway. Pass through it and climb straight ahead up a groove beside a field. A grassy track leads up to the farm of **Merry Know**. Keep just to the right of the buildings, crossing stone step-stiles over walls between a couple of yards. Leave the farm by following a field path, lining up stiles and gates while heading downhill to reach a minor road.

Cross the road and cross a ladder stile, then head up through a field to cross another ladder stile. Walk across a couple of fields, then down stone steps. Go through an arch under a railway viaduct to reach a house and the A689 road at **Burnstones**. ◀ Turn left to follow the road across a river and back through another arch under the railway viaduct. An access road for **Knarsdale Hall** is reached, where the Pennine Way is signposted through a gateway into a small parking space.

Climb up through a kissing gate into a field, and head for the top corner of the field to go through another kissing

Map continued on page 165

The Kirkstyle Inn is signposted off-route at Knarsdale, and offers food and drink.

gate. Turn right to follow a track uphill until the Pennine Way is signposted off to the right, above **Side House**, and there is a distant view of The Cheviot. A vague path leads down a rushy slope, then turn left along a broad, boggy, rushy old track. This is the Roman road of **Maiden Way** and it becomes drier later, passing through a gate, gaining a stony surface. However, the stony track bends uphill, so fork right, straight ahead, across a rushy slope to pass through another gate. Further along, cross a ladder stile and a step-stile over two fences close together.

Knarsdale Hall, where the Pennine Way shifts onto the course of the Maiden Way Roman road

MAIDEN WAY

It is possible that the Romans penetrated the North Pennines in search of its mineral riches, but no-one knows for sure, nor does anyone know if they had names for their roads. *Maydengathe* was the name of this route in an abbey record of 1179. William Camden, writing in his book *Britannica*, which was published in 1586, mentioned 'a street called Mayden Way, which is paved with stones throughout the moors, about some forty miles in length.'

A narrow path continues between a drystone wall and a fence along a broad, grassy, rushy strip of moorland. At first the path is beside the wall, heading over a gentle rise and downhill, but the wall and fence both drift away later. Cross a step-stile over a fence, and although a road bend is in view ahead, keep well to the left to miss it and cross a footbridge over **Glendue Burn**. Cross a step-stile over a fence and climb uphill to the right, following the fence and a drystone wall between a patch of woodland and a heather moor. Cross a stone step-stile and continue to follow the wall uphill. There is grass and bracken on this side of the wall, with plenty of rushes later, while on the other side there is a grass and heather moor mixed with mossy bog.

Cross a step-stile over an adjoining fence and continue over a rushy crest at almost 300m (985ft) on **Lambley Common**. The drystone wall ends suddenly. Cross another step-stile over an adjoining fence and continue walking straight ahead, now using a fence as a guide. The ground is very boggy at first, with rushes and squelchy moss, but it gets firmer and starts to descend gently. Cross yet another step-stile over an adjoining fence.

Follow the fence down a rushy slope and cross a final step-stile over an adjoining fence. Continue down a gentle, grassy, rushy slope where a track forms underfoot. This leads down to a road and a house, but the Pennine Way doesn't go that far. Instead, turn left across a step-stile over the fence, as indicated by an 'acorn' marker. Walk along a narrow path across a heather and bilberry moor. The path becomes vague, so drift downhill to the right, reaching the **A689 road** where there is a step-stile over a fence and a Pennine Way signpost.

Cross over the road and cross a ladder stile over a drystone wall, also signposted for the Pennine Way. Follow a wall down and across a grassy, rushy area. ◀ When the wall levels out and turns left, leave it and cross a stone-slab footbridge over **Black Burn**. Walk straight up a vague path on a gently sloping grass and rushy moor. A few stretches of flagstones cross boggy patches, then a marker stone on a little hump of spoil indicates a drift to the right.

Most of what lies to the right was formerly a coal mine and the grassy slope is all colliery spoil.

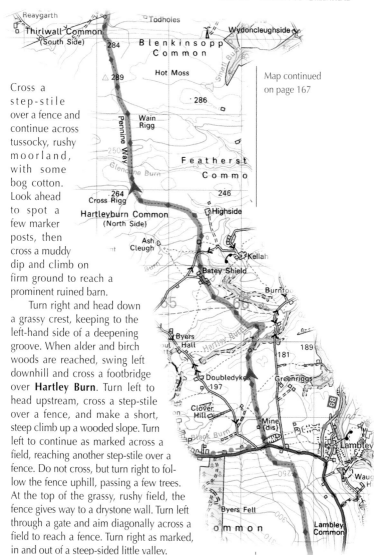

Map continued
on page 167

Cross a step-stile over a fence and continue across tussocky, rushy moorland, with some bog cotton. Look ahead to spot a few marker posts, then cross a muddy dip and climb on firm ground to reach a prominent ruined barn.

Turn right and head down a grassy crest, keeping to the left-hand side of a deepening groove. When alder and birch woods are reached, swing left downhill and cross a footbridge over **Hartley Burn**. Turn left to head upstream, cross a step-stile over a fence, and make a short, steep climb up a wooded slope. Turn left to continue as marked across a field, reaching another step-stile over a fence. Do not cross, but turn right to follow the fence uphill, passing a few trees. At the top of the grassy, rushy field, the fence gives way to a drystone wall. Turn left through a gate and aim diagonally across a field to reach a fence. Turn right as marked, in and out of a steep-sided little valley.

Follow the fence towards the farm at **Batey Shield**, where there are lots of outbuildings. On reaching these, turn right to go through a gate in a wall, then turn left along a track to pass between some of the outbuildings. Go through a gate on the right, marked with an 'acorn', to keep right of the farmhouse. Walk down a field and cross a footbridge over **Kellah Burn**, then immediately cross a minor road and walk straight up a track. Go through a gate and pass just to the left of a cottage, then cross a ladder stile.

Take care from this point, first climbing straight up through a field, with barely a trace of a path. Watch carefully to spot the top of a ladder stile over a fence, lost among rushes at the top of the field. Once across, continue along a narrow path across the rushy moor of **Hartleyburn Common**. Gradually, this begins to drift left, but be careful not to drift too far left. The correct line follows a sort of broad, high crest, avoiding rushy, boggy hollows, to reach a marker post beside a fence, at almost 250m (820ft).

After passing a house to reach Hartleyburn Common, careful route-finding is required to reach Wain Rigg

Turn right to follow the fence, which runs down onto a level, squelchy bog and crosses a little footbridge.

Climb uphill beside the fence, over a rise and down into another boggy dip. The fence leads to a drystone wall, which is crossed using a ladder stile flanked by duck-boards. Climb uphill on a grassy, tussocky moor, veering left to reach another fence. Climb further uphill on **Wain Rigg**, possibly spotting a ruin across the fence. Leave the fence at a corner and follow the path across undulating, boggy moorland. Keep to the path no matter how much it wriggles and writhes, to reach a ladder stile over a dry-stone wall. There is a trig point to the left, at 289m (948ft), but this isn't visited. Walk across the boggy moorland of **Blenkinsopp Common**.

Walk downhill to cross a step-stile over a fence, then head down a pathless slope to reach two ruined brick buildings. Pass to the right of them, going under a power line at the same time. Go down a path on a grassy embankment and cross a stone-slab footbridge to reach a gate. Turn right as signposted to follow a stony, grassy track gently up through a big field, passing under the power line again. Pass a little stone hut at **Todholes** and cross a ladder stile beside a gate.

Follow the grassy track up a rushy slope and it later drops a bit and runs alongside a fence, reaching a junction with another track. Turn left down through a gate, as signposted for the Pennine Way. The track follows a fence across a rushy moor, passing through

Map continued from page 165

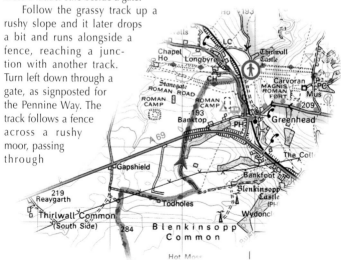

another gate and running beneath the power line again. Lines of beech flank the track, then after passing through a gate a birch wood is passed as the track runs down to the busy **A69 road**.

Cross the road with care to find the Pennine Way signposted a short way downhill on the right. Climb a flight of steps, cross a step-stile over a fence, go through a gate in another fence, then head diagonally right to reach the far corner of a field. Cross a step-stile over a fence, quickly followed by a ladder stile over a drystone wall. Follow the wall downhill beside a small mixed woodland, continuing down beside a golf course. The route climbs a short way uphill before it is signposted left, over a ladder stile onto the golf course.

Keep to the right of a strip of rumpled rough grassland, where the Roman earthwork known as the **Vallum** runs across the golf course. Cross a footbridge in a slight dip. A steep and overgrown path drops down to a ladder stile, reaching the **B6318 road** at a short terrace of houses. At this point, the Pennine Way and Hadrian's Wall National Trails coincide, and while both routes can be followed straight across the road, this is far enough for the day. Turn right along the road to reach the little village of **Greenhead**.

GREENHEAD

Facilities are limited in Greenhead, and they come under a lot of pressure from people walking along Hadrian's Wall. The Greenhead Hotel, a youth hostel and Ye Olde Forge Tearooms are in the village. There is a campsite nearby, while Holmhead Farm Guest House also offers a camping barn. In case of difficulty securing accommodation, the Hadrian's Wall bus and other bus services offer links with Haltwhistle, Brampton, Carlisle and Newcastle.

DAY 16
Greenhead to Housesteads

Start	Greenhead Hotel, NY 660 654
Finish	Military Road, Housesteads, NY 793 683
Distance	12km (7½ miles)
Ascent	550m (1805ft)
Descent	450m (1475ft)
Maps	OS Landranger 86, OS Explorer OL43, Harvey's Pennine Way North
Terrain	A roller-coaster route with several short, steep ascents and descents. Paths are usually obvious and some steep slopes feature steps.
Refreshments	Cafés and snacks available at Thirlwall and Walltown. Pubs off-route at Cawfields and Twice Brewed. Café at Housesteads.

This is only a short day's walk, but it proves quite fascinating and there is much to see. Ensure that you have plenty of time to visit a couple of museums. Bear in mind that Hadrian's Wall can get very busy and all the nearby accommodation can be fully booked at peak periods. The walk lies within the Northumberland National Park and is something of a roller-coaster, running along the crest of the rugged Whin Sill. Some walkers aim to cover the distance between Greenhead and Bellingham in a day.

Blocky dolerite cliffs rises proudly above Crag Lough as the route continues towards Hotbank

HADRIAN'S WALL

In AD122 the Emperor Hadrian ordered the building of this remarkable coast-to-coast fortification, and it took eight years to complete. Large forts were built at intervals, with milecastles every Roman mile, equating to 1481m (1620yds). Between each milecastle were two small turrets. Roman miles are counted from east to west and the turrets are labelled A and B. There are gaps in the numbering system where fortifications have been destroyed.

The Venerable Bede noted 'it is eight feet in breadth, and twelve in height; and, as can be clearly seen to this day, ran straight from east to west'. Interest in the wall increased from the 16th century, due in part to curiosity generated by William Camden's *Britannica*. General Wade's construction of the 'Military Road' in the 1750s made Hadrian's Wall more accessible, though much of the masonry was destroyed to lay the foundations of the road. In 1801, at the age of 78, William Hutton explored Hadrian's Wall in a remarkable 965km (600 mile) round trip on foot from Birmingham. The Rev. John Hodgson published the first detailed description of the wall in 1840. The archaeologist J Collingwood Bruce led the first 'pilgrimage' along the wall in 1849, and such 'pilgrimages' continue to this day.

Some 32km (20 miles) of the best stretches of Hadrian's Wall were included in the Northumberland National Park when it was designated 1956. After a lengthy period of consultation, the course of Hadrian's Wall was designated as a National Trail in the year 2000 and is also a World Heritage Site.

Start by following the road from **Greenhead**, signposted for Gilsland, back to the little terrace of houses and the junction of the Pennine Way and Hadrian's Wall National Trails. Turn right in front of the terrace, cross a railway line at a level crossing, cross a footbridge over a stream, and cross a cycleway, all close together. Follow a grassy path onwards, bending left, to reach a track below the 14th-century ruins of **Thirlwall Castle**. Either climb to the

Map continued
on page 172

castle and explore, or turn right along the track and cross a footbridge over a stream.

Pass Holmhead Farm Guest House, which also offers a camping barn and refreshments. Follow the track uphill, bending left to go up through a gate. Walk up a grassy slope beside a prominent ditch associated with Hadrian's Wall, though all the stone was robbed to build Thirlwall Castle. Cross a ladder stile over a drystone wall and the ground levels out, with a view back to Cross Fell. Walk downhill a little to a reach a kissing gate and minor road. Turn right as signposted 'National Trails'. Either turn left for **Walltown** quarry, or walk straight along the road a bit further for the Roman Army Museum.

WALLTOWN

An old whinstone quarry now serves as a picnic site. There is a small shop offering basic refreshments, and the Hadrian's Wall bus turns in the car park. The Roman Army Museum is nearby, and also has a café, though this is only available to paying visitors (tel: 01434 344277, **www.vindolanda.com**). Walltown Lodge B&B is opposite the museum.

Leave the quarry by following paths marked with the 'acorn' symbol. Keep well to the left of the flooded quarry bottom, then pass below the tallest quarried rock face. The path leads up to a gate and a left turn leads up to a splendid stretch of Hadrian's Wall. Turn right to follow it above **Walltown Crags**. There are extensive views

One of the tallest stretches of Hadrian's Wall is seen where it traverses Walltown Crags

back to the Pennines and ahead across the border forests into southern Scotland. The wall is tall and well-built, rising and falling on the crest, leading to the square base of **Turret 45A**. The wall ends where it was destroyed by another quarry.

The next stretch of the wall is represented only by a hummocky ridge of tumbled masonry, and it is easy to pass the site of Milecastle 45 without realising. Walk down to a gap and cross a ladder stile over a drystone

Map continued on page 175

wall. Note how the Romans dug a ditch across the gap, creating an extra defence across a vulnerable low area. A flagstone path and stone steps lead uphill and **Turret 44B** is passed. The wall along the crest has completely collapsed.

Cross another gap, where there is another stile over a wall. Climb past low rocky outcrops, and note that the path misses the crest, where another tumbled stretch of the old wall can be followed. Cross a ladder stile over another wall and head downhill. Low stretches of Hadrian's Wall can be seen. A drystone wall was built on top in 2009 to aid conservation. Walk onwards, crossing a track and later crossing a ladder stile over a wall. Follow a gravel path through mixed woodland, climbing another ladder stile to leave it, passing a house.

Walk through a field and cross a ladder stile into another field. Ahead is the farm of **Great Chesters**, where the grassy ramparts of the Roman fort of Aesica can be explored. ▶ Cross a couple more ladder stiles while walking gently downhill through fields, passing a few low stretches of Hadrian's Wall, incorporated into a drystone wall. Pass a gate and ladder stile, then walk down through a field to pass Burnhead B&B. Cross a stone step-stile and turn right along a minor road. Cross a bridge over a stream and turn left along a road, then right into **Cawfields** quarry. ▶

A 'National Trails' sign indicates a path keeping left of the flooded quarry bottom, leading up to a gate in a gap. Turn left to inspect **Milecastle 42**, which has chunky stone gateways. A fine stretch of Hadrian's Wall can be followed up and down along a grassy crest. The wall is continuous, except where a farm gate has been installed. Climb stone steps and walk along the crest, then drop into a dip and climb more stone steps back onto the crest. Cross a step-stile over a fence then pass the low base of **Turret 41A**. A low wall runs down to a gate onto a minor road at Caw Gap, near **Shield on the Wall**.

Cross the road and go through a gate, climbing stone steps to continue following a drystone wall. Walk along the crest and down to a gap, then climb steeply. There

Features include a well beneath a stone arch, and a Roman altar covered with assorted coins.

The Milecastle Inn is located only 10 minutes off-route on the B6318 road.

A splendid stretch of Hadrian's Wall gradually climbs towards the top of Winshields Crag

Views are extensive, with the North Pennines dominated by Cross Fell and Cold Fell. Parts of southern Scotland and the border forests are seen, and the humps of the Cheviot Hills rise beyond.

Anyone planning to stay at the Once Brewed youth hostel or Twice Brewed Inn should walk off-route to the B6318 road.

are a couple of lesser ups and downs, then after passing a gate in a drystone wall, climb uphill again. A stretch of Hadrian's Wall runs along the top, merging almost seamlessly with a drystone wall built from the old Roman masonry. Follow this wall down to a gap and go through a gate in a wall, then climb uphill on rocky ground, which gives way to a gentler crest. A signpost points right, off-route to Winshields campsite and tearoom. If these are not required, keep walking ahead to reach a trig point at 345m (1132ft) on **Winshields Crag**, the highest point on Hadrian's Wall. ◄

Follow the crest onwards and the drystone wall gives way to a short stretch of Hadrian's Wall. Further downhill, only the low base of the original wall survives, with a drystone wall on top of it. A grassy path leads down through a small and a large gate, then a stone step-stile leads onto a minor road. ◄

Cross a stone step-stile to leave the road and walk, for a change, along the northern side of Hadrian's Wall. Go through a small gate and walk downhill, using a flagstone

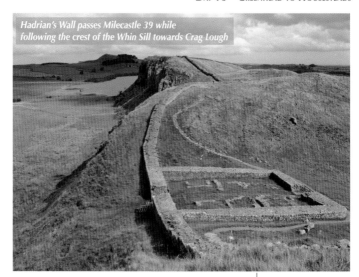

Hadrian's Wall passes Milecastle 39 while following the crest of the Whin Sill towards Crag Lough

path to cross a gap. Unseen on the other side of the wall is the curious Turret 39AB. ▶ Climb steep stone steps beside the dramatic cliffs of **Steel Rigg**. Cross a ladder stile over a wall and continue along an easy gravel path. A good stretch of Hadrian's Wall runs along the crest and down to a gap.

Cross a ladder stile over a wall and climb uphill, now following only the tumbled remains of the old wall. However, an iconic stretch of Hadrian's Wall appears later, where the path features steps to drop down to a gap, passing **Milecastle 39**, then climb up the other side.

Lying between the sites of 39A and 39B, Turret 39AB is the exception to the 'rule' for the spacing of turrets.

Map continued on page 176

175

Map continued
from page 175

Old shielings
are passed on the
crest, then steep stone steps
drop down to Sycamore Gap, another
iconic scene on the wall. Cross Hadrian's Wall and climb
up stone steps, then cross a ladder stile at the end of
the old wall. An easy gravel path runs beside tumbled
masonry, overlooking the attractive **Crag Lough**. Rowans
cling to the cliffs, then the path passes through a plantation of Scots pine and sycamore. Cross a ladder stile and
note the willow growing at the head of the lake.

A ladder stile leads onto a track on a gentle gap, then
a gate takes the path onwards, beside a drystone wall.
The path is broad and grassy, rising gently beside tumbled masonry to pass the grassy ramparts of Milecastle
38 opposite a farm at **Hotbank**. Cross a ladder stile
over a fence and climb steeply. Pick up and follow a
long stretch of Hadrian's Wall along an undulating crest
above **Hotbank Crags**. A drystone wall drops down to
Rapishaw Gap, where the Pennine Way parts company
with Hadrian's Wall. However, it is well worth making a
detour further along the wall to Housesteads, as follows.

Cross a ladder stile over a wall, then climb up a short,
rocky slope to pick up another good stretch of Hadrian's
Wall. Follow it over a hill, then down and up stone steps
to cross yet another iconic gap. Pass **Milecastle 37** and
follow the wall onwards, though a gate in a wall, along a
path through a sycamore wood. Emerge at the corner of
the Roman fort at **Housesteads**, and go through a gate on
the right to reach a nearby museum. The exterior of the
fort can be enjoyed free, but there is an entry charge to
explore the interior.

HOUSESTEADS ROMAN FORT

This site has a long and complex history, with notable gaps. Bronze Age farming settlements were cleared during the construction of Hadrian's Wall. Housesteads, known to the Romans as Vercovicium, was probably garrisoned by 500 men. The fort was abandoned at the end of the 4th century. There is no evidence of settlement at Housesteads until 1326, and even then there were only summer shielings. Permanent settlement was probably inadvisable due to border strife. William Camden didn't visit Housesteads when researching his book *Britannica*, declaring 'I would not with safetie take the full survey of it for the rankie-robbers thereabouts'.

Some excavation work was done at Housesteads in 1849, but work to restore Hadrian's Wall commenced in earnest from 1908. Housesteads Fort was given to the National Trust by JM Clayton in 1930, and the Trust has since acquired other properties in the area.

Follow a broad gravel track away from Housesteads, rising and falling and finally climbing to reach an information centre, café and car park beside the **B6318**, or 'Military Road'. Accommodation is sparse hereabouts, but the Hadrian's Wall bus can be used to reach lodgings lying further afield.

Housesteads is one of the finest Roman forts on Hadrian's Wall and is well worth visiting

DAY 17

Housesteads to Bellingham

Start	Military Road, Housesteads, NY 793 683
Finish	Town Hall, Bellingham, NY 838 833
Distance	23km (14 miles)
Ascent	380m (1245ft)
Descent	500m (1640ft)
Maps	OS Landranger 80 and 86, OS Explorer OL42 and OL43, Harvey's Pennine Way North
Terrain	Low moorlands, forest tracks and paths, along with field paths and farm tracks. There are some wet, boggy or muddy patches. Careful route-finding is required at times.
Refreshments	Plenty of choice around Bellingham.

Once the Pennine Way leaves Hadrian's Wall, it becomes very quiet. It is possible to walk all the way to Bellingham without meeting another walker, and even if some are met, they will be Pennine Wayfarers. There are extensive areas of forest, as areas of open moorland, farmland and fields. On the latter half of the day's walk, the course of the Pennine Way is actually the boundary of the Northumberland National Park. The land on the left is inside the park, while the land on the right is outside it, though it all looks the same! At the end of the day, Bellingham is the last little town with a full range of services.

Assuming that a diversion was made to Housesteads, the first task is to return to the Pennine Way. Start on the **B6318 road** at the information centre and follow the clear gravel path through fields to reach **Housesteads**. Keep just to the left of the fort, climbing past the museum, to find a small gate in a wall. Go through and turn left to follow a path up through a strip of sycamore woodland, walking parallel to Hadrian's Wall. Leave the wood at another gate and follow the wall along a crest, passing **Milecastle 37**.

Walk down stone steps to a gap, then up the other side. Remember to look back before leaving the gap, as this is one of the most popular views on Hadrian's Wall. Continue along the crest then head left as marked, as the wall ends abruptly above a small cliff. Turn right to reach a ladder stile crossing over a wall on Rapishaw Gap. Almost immediately, another ladder stile crosses a wall on the right, where the Pennine Way is signposted north, away from Hadrian's Wall.

There are two grassy paths, and the Pennine Way is the one crossing a huge field diagonally. Follow it down into a rushy dip where there are flagstones, then up to a gate in a wall. On the other side there are two grassy tracks, so keep left and head down into another rushy dip to cross a stream, with a view of **Broomlee Lough** far to the right. Walk up to a gate in another wall, go through and follow a fine grassy track across another broad dip in a rushy, tussocky moorland, crossing **Jenkins Burn**. Rise gently uphill to cross a heathery crest, then head gently downhill and fork left to reach a gate and signposts beside a track near the ruins of **Cragend**.

Looking back along a flagstone path towards Rapishaw Gap while crossing broad moorlands

Don't be tempted off-route towards a footbridge and a farm.

Cross the track and watch for a series of marker posts. These indicate a path bending left downhill, with a view of **Greenlee Lough**. Cross a muddy, rushy area with some firm flagstones underfoot. Head gently uphill and drift right as marked. ◄ Drift left downhill to reach a rushy dip to cross a wall. Cross a footbridge, then drift left up a grassy slope to spot a tall, stout wooded post bearing acorn markers. Cross a ladder stile beside a gate in a wall, then walk down to a track near the farm of **East Stonefolds**.

Turn right to follow the track up through a gate and into a forest. Climb gently with an open moorland on the right and trees on the left, crossing a crest where there are trees on both sides. The track runs down into a dip where open moorland lies on the left and trees on the right, then climbs with trees on both sides. When signposts appear on the right, the Pennine Way leaves the track and veers right to follow a squelchy forest ride. Pass a little clearing and eventually reach a step-stile over the forest fence.

Map continued on page 181

Wet, boggy, tussocky moorland is crossed near **Hawk Side**. The path is fairly obvious and direct throughout. There is a dip in the middle of the moor, with a step-stile and a gate in a fence, with a footbridge just beyond. Later, keep left of a small, stone-walled enclosure containing a few pines and birch. The path leads to a gate to enter another area of forest. Follow a direct path through the forest, crossing a track, then later turn right along a track, then turn left down a path. Tracks are crossed two more times before the path levels out beside a wall at the edge of the forest. Cross a step-

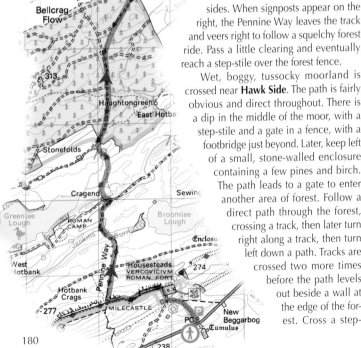

stile and walk straight ahead over a grassy, rushy moor with some bog cotton, keeping to the left of a tumbled wall and fence.

Turn right to follow a minor road uphill, passing the access road for **Willowbog**, which grows bonsai, to reach the access road for **Ladyhill**, a falconry centre. Turn left down a path between a wall and a forest. ▶ Cross a road and follow a level path, then cross a track. The path rises beside a forest then there are trees on both sides before a gate is used to leave the forest. The path leading onwards down a tussocky moorland slope can be vague, especially in mist. Avoid being drawn along other trodden paths, but the only real landmark is an old white stone sink! Pass this and continue down to the small stream of **Fawlee Sike**.

Climb up to the corner of a drystone wall. Keep right of the wall to cross a crest, then head straight downhill keeping to the left of a fence. When a drystone wall and a gate are reached, turn right as signposted for the Pennine Way, and pass to the right of a ramshackle corrugated barn. Walk through bracken and watch for a path down to the left

Turn left along the road if a basic campsite at Stonehaugh is required.

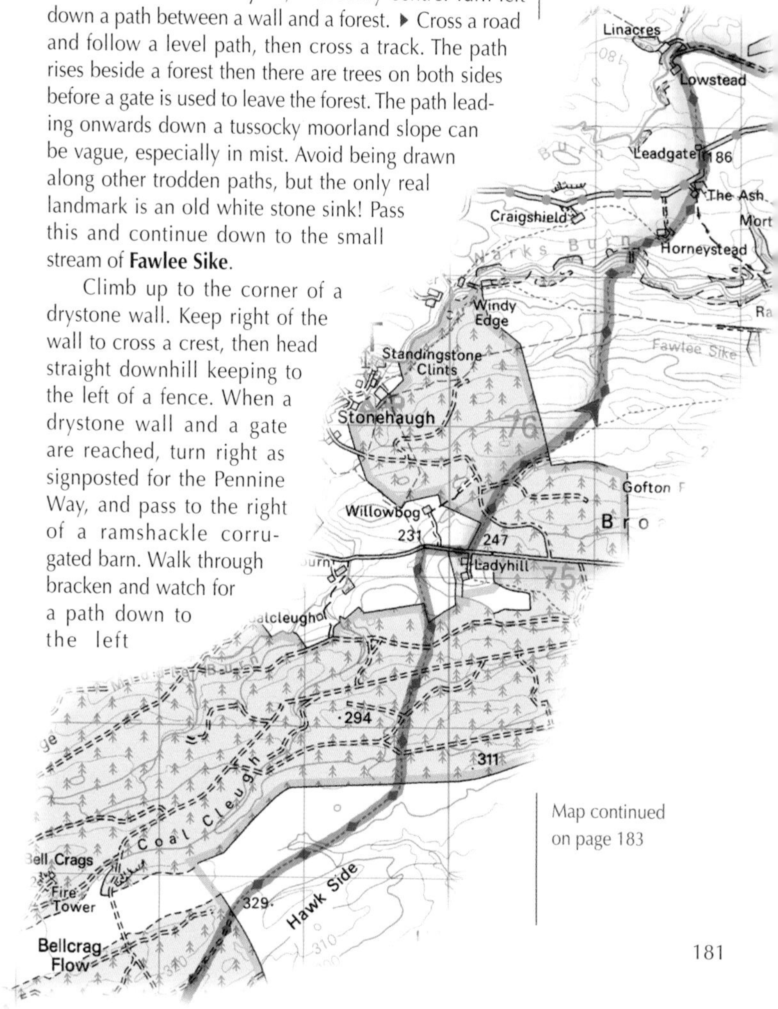

Map continued on page 183

181

into a valley. **Warks Burn** cannot be seen, because it is cut deep into the bedrock and flanked by trees. Look carefully to find a footbridge and cross to the other side.

A path climbs from the burn, swinging left up a slope of bracken, then right to reach a grassy brow. A field path leads up to a step-stile over a fence then passes the farm of **Horneystead**. Line up other stiles and gates to pass the farmhouse called **The Ash**. Turn left to cross a dip where there is a stone step-stile over a wall. Aim to the right of a house at **Leadgate**, crossing a minor road to pass it.

Walk down into a field and cross a wall into another field. Cross a dip and climb uphill, keeping right of tall ash trees. Keep right of the attractive house and gardens of **Lowstead** as marked, turning a succession of little corners to reach its access road. Turn right to follow this away from the house, across a cattle grid, and keep straight ahead along a road to cross another cattle grid. When a triangular road junction is reached, turn left uphill. ◄ Follow the road downhill to cross yet another cattle grid. The road is enclosed by walls and hawthorns as it descends past fields to reach another road junction.

Turning right quickly leads to a farmhouse B&B at Hetherington.

Walk straight ahead through fields and down towards **Houxty Burn**, but take care on the last part of the descent.

Walkers approach the attractive house of Lowstead and will leave along its access road

A signpost might be spotted in the bottom corner of the field, but this is for a ford. There is a footbridge further upstream, but this can't be seen on the descent. Locate it and cross it, then turn right downstream, and cross another footbridge over an inflowing stream. Turn left through a gate and follow a track that bends right as it climbs up to the farm of **Shitlington Hall**.

Pass the farm and turn left behind it along a field track. This later turns right through a gate and expires, so walk uphill along the edge of a field. There is a slight dip where a step-stile crosses a fence beside **Slade Sike** to enter the next field. Climb again and cross a ladder stile over a wall to reach a track. Note that a bunkhouse is available at the farm on the right. The Pennine Way crosses the track and climbs straight uphill, bending left where a broad path has been hammered out of the low gritstone edge of **Shitlington Crags**.

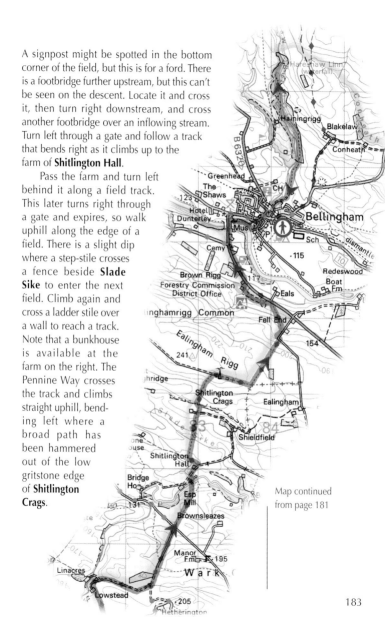

Map continued from page 181

183

Watch out for tall marker posts across the top of Ealingham Rigg above North Tynedale

A marker post shows the Pennine Way heading straight up a gentle, rushy moorland slope, reaching a narrow road. Turn right to follow this towards a prominent tall mast on **Ealingham Rigg**, over 230m (755ft). Continue straight ahead, gently down a grassy track beside a wall. A marker post indicates a left turn across a rushy moor. The path is vague, so look for more marker posts, which reveal a couple of footbridges over boggy patches. Walk down a grassy slope and cross a ladder stile onto a minor road. Turn left along the road, which suddenly turns right downhill.

Watch for a ladder stile on the left and cross a wall into a field. A path appears to head down towards the **B6320 road**, but doesn't immediately join it. Instead, keep off the road until later, and even then there is a path running beside it as far as a caravan site at **Brown Rigg**. Follow the road onwards to cross a four-arched bridge over the **River North Tyne**. Go down steps on the right to follow a short riverside path, then follow a road up into the centre of **Bellingham**.

BELLINGHAM

The name is pronounced 'Bellinjam' and the village is surprisingly busy, serving a large rural area. Facilites include a couple of hotels and B&Bs, a bunkhouse and campsites. There are two banks, one with an ATM, while the post office also has an ATM. There are shops, a couple of pubs and a café. Buses run to and from Hexham, except Sundays, and there are also buses to Kielder. A tourist information centre is available (tel: 01434 220616). This shares the same building as the Heritage Centre, for which there is an entry fee (tel: 01434 220050, **www.bellingham-heritage.org.uk**).

Off-route to Hareshaw Linn

In its earliest days, the Pennine Way left Bellingham by way of a splendid waterfall called Hareshaw Linn, reached by a popular path through a wonderfully wooded gorge.

The lovely waterfall of Hareshaw Linn used to be on the Pennine Way and is well worth a visit

Unfortunately, there has been no link between the waterfall and the Pennine Way for decades, but anyone with a couple of hours to spare could complete a there-and-back walk measuring 5km (3 miles).

Start at the police station in **Bellingham**, where a road opposite is signposted for Hareshaw Linn. The road runs upstream beside **Hareshaw Burn** and gives way to a track rising past a caravan site. This in turn gives way to a fine path that works its way through dense woodlands with a rampant understorey, featuring flights of stone steps. Seven footbridges are crossed before **Hareshaw Linn** is finally reached, cascading down a multi-layered rock-face into a deep pool. Retrace your footsteps to Bellingham.

DAY 18
Bellingham to Byrness

Start	Town Hall, Bellingham, NY 838 833
Finish	Byrness Church, NT 771 024
Distance	26km (16 miles)
Ascent	550m (1805ft)
Descent	450m (1475ft)
Maps	OS Landranger 80, OS Explorer OL16 and OL42, Harvey's Pennine Way North
Terrain	Farmland quickly gives way to rolling heather moorland, with increasingly boggy patches. A firm track allows rapid progress through extensive forest.
Refreshments	Café at Byrness.

This is a bleak and remote day, passing very few habitations. After leaving Bellingham, fields give way to broad and gently rolling heather moorland. There are extensive views in fine weather, but in foul weather it is simply a treadmill. There are plenty of soft and wet bogs later, getting progressively worse until a huge forest is reached. At that point, with a firm and dry track underfoot, it is possible to stride out and make rapid progress to Byrness.

Starting from the Town Hall in **Bellingham**, follow the Main Street as far as the two banks. Turn right to cross a bridge over **Hareshaw Burn** and later keep left as signposted for West Woodburn. The road climbs past the Heritage Centre and tourist information centre, which are both on the site of a former railway station. Pass a caravan park to leave the village and climb further up the road. Turn left along a narrow, tarmac farm access road, passing through gates to reach **Blakelaw Farm**.

Turn left to walk through the farmyard and go through a gate into an enormous field. There is no trodden path, so look ahead to spot signposts and marker posts. Reach a gate in a wall, well to the right of a plantation of Scots pine. There are wide-ranging views around Northumberland,

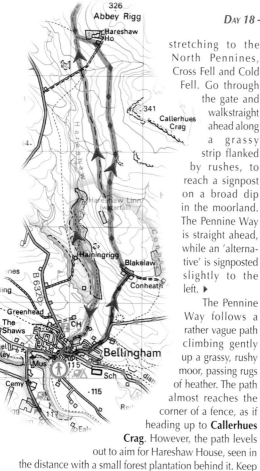

Map continued
on page 188

stretching to the North Pennines, Cross Fell and Cold Fell. Go through the gate and walk straight ahead along a grassy strip flanked by rushes, to reach a signpost on a broad dip in the moorland. The Pennine Way is straight ahead, while an 'alternative' is signposted slightly to the left. ▶

The Pennine Way follows a rather vague path climbing gently up a grassy, rushy moor, passing rugs of heather. The path almost reaches the corner of a fence, as if heading up to **Callerhues Crag**. However, the path levels out to aim for Hareshaw House, seen in the distance with a small forest plantation behind it. Keep to the right of a circular drystone sheepfold, which is a handy feature once the distant house is lost to view.

Extensive areas of heather and bracken are passed on the moor, as well as bog cotton. The path becomes more obvious and is unlikely to be lost. It drifts downhill and uphill and can be wet and boggy in places. Pass to the right of a band of tall Scots pine. Go through a gate and cross a footbridge over a small stream then head straight

The alternative route follows a fence and a drystone wall across the moorland slope, crosses a minor road, then follows another drystone wall straight ahead to rejoin the main route.

The 'garden' in front of the house is often a bed of nettles and many walkers detour through other nearby gates.

Map continued on page 191

for a gate onto a minor road. Turn right, then left to pass in front of a derelict house. ◀

Walk across a small field below **Hareshaw House** and cross a ladder stile beside a gate. A grassy track runs down a field towards a solitary sycamore tree, to reach another ladder stile beside a gate. Follow a grassy track across a rushy moorland slope. Walk straight ahead down a clearer track, noticing old colliery spoil on both sides of a road. Go through gates to cross the **B6320 road**, then of all the vague paths in view, follow one that keeps just to the left of a small hump of colliery spoil.

The path is vague across a grassy, rushy moor, but a marker post points towards a gentle slope where it becomes more obvious through heather. The route misses the summit of **Lough Shaw** then crosses a broad dip. Marker posts show the way up to the summit of **Deer Play**, where a cairn and signpost stand at 361m (1184ft). A gentle descent leads across a broad and boggy dip then the path becomes firm and grassy as it climbs to the heathery summit of **Lord's Shaw**, where a cairn stands at 356m (1168ft). Cross a step-stile over a fence, then head right to pick up a worn, peaty path down a heathery slope. A level flagstone path is slowly sinking into a bog on the way to a minor road crossing a gap.

379 Monument
Pennine Way
Padon Hill
330 350

Keeper's
Cott
325

Whitley Pike
356 Cairn
Lord's Shaw

T r o u

Deer Play
361

. 336

Lough Shaw

326
Abbey Rigg

Hareshaw
Ho

*Pennine Wayfarers head from Lough Shaw towards
Padon Hill across broad heather moorlands*

Cross the road and follow a firm path uphill, which often proves awkwardly stony underfoot, following a fence and passing a prominent little outcrop of rock. A steeper climb is followed by a walk along a gently undulating crest. Cross a level boggy patch using a flagstone path. A conspicuous 'pepperpot' cairn stands just off-route, at 379m (1243ft) on **Padon Hill**. It can be approached by a short detour.

PADON HILL

Alexander Peden was a 17th-century Scottish Covenanter, who preached in remote locations to avoid persecution. Padon Hill is named after him and a story tells how every worshipper who gathered on the hill was required to bring one stone with them to make a cairn. Much of the old cairn was subsequently re-used to make the stout 'pepperpot' cairn which dates from the 1920s.

The stout 'pepperpot' cairn on Padon Hill can be reached by a short detour from the Pennine Way

The path beside the fence heads down a heathery slope to reach a wall. Cross a ladder stile and follow a flagstone path across a flat bog where bog asphodel

grows. Cross a step-stile over a fence and climb uphill beside a forest, following a tumbled wall and a fence. The climb is steep and muddy at times and may rank as one of the worst stretches of the Pennine Way. Cross a step-stile over a fence at the top and follow a wall away from the forest, climbing gently across heather moorland. The wall meets a fence on **Brownrigg Head** at 365m (1198ft).

Turn left to follow a fence, which separates heather moorland from grassy moorland. It can be wet and boggy underfoot. A line of boundary stones bearing the letters 'GH' occur at intervals. ▶ Cross a broad and boggy dip then rise very gently over **Black Hill**. The fence runs back towards the forest then later there is forest on both sides. The path reaches a firm track at a gate beside a Forestry Commission sign, at 347m (1138ft).

These were planted to mark the estate of Gabriel Hall, High Sheriff of Northumberland, in 1705.

Turn right to pass through the gate and follow the track downhill. Two tracks join from the left, then the Pennine Way is signposted off to the left. Think twice before following it, since it

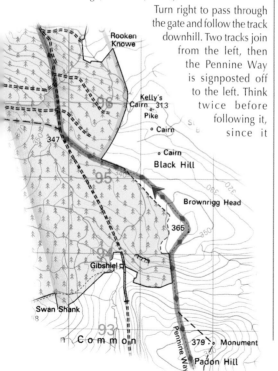

Map continued on page 192

191

Map continued
from page 191

merely runs parallel to the track, but on a rather rough vegetated slope where the path dwindles away completely. In fact, many who take this path quickly head back to the track. There is another sign at the bottom, but little evidence of a trodden path. Follow the track uphill from a dip, passing another track that joins from the left. Climb straight uphill to a crest at 296m (971ft), where there is a grassy short-cut on the left.

Follow the track onwards, passing a track joining from the left. After a gentle ascent and descent, pass a track joining from the right, then pass another one joining from the left. The track simply runs straight ahead and downhill, leaving the

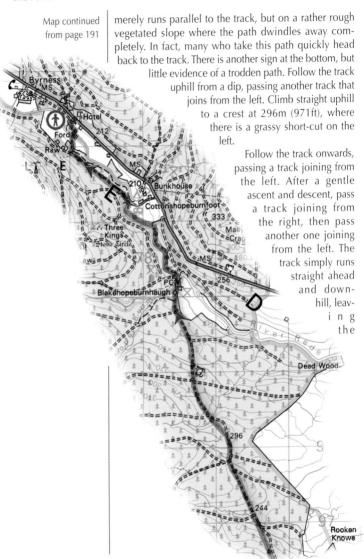

192

forest briefly to pass a house at **Blakehopeburnhaugh**, which happens to be the longest place-name on the Pennine Way! Pass a toilet block and turn right along a road, crossing a bridge over the **River Rede**. Turn left as signposted for the Pennine Way, along a forest track. There are tall trees here and the track gives way to a pleasant, grassy riverside path.

Simply follow the river upstream until it can be crossed by a bridge at **Cottonshopeburn Foot**, where there is a campsite. Follow the track past fields and back into the forest. Turn right at a track junction, heading down and out of the forest to a ford and footbridge. Walk up the track and turn right at a junction, reaching the **A68 road** beside a small church at **Byrness**.

BYRNESS

Byrness is a tiny place, made up of a few buildings near a little church, and a nearby huddle of buildings originally housing workers employed in the construction of Catcleugh Reservoir. The houses were then acquired by the Forestry Commission, and two of them were converted into a youth hostel.

Facilities are sparse at Byrness and accommodation is limited to The Byrness B&B, near the church and garage, and Forest View youth hostel, in the forestry village. The garage operates a café and also sells sweets and drinks, while the hostel has a small food store. There is a very limited bus service, basically one bus per day linking Byrness with Jedburgh and Newcastle, and seats must be booked in advance. Another bus runs on Tuesday to Hexham.

DAY 19
Byrness to Clennell Street

Start	Byrness Church, NT 771 024
Finish	Clennell Street, NT 871 160
Distance	23km (14 miles)
Ascent	820m (2690ft)
Descent	500m (1640ft)
Maps	OS Landranger 80, OS Explorer OL16, Harvey's Pennine Way North
Terrain	Broad, high and exposed boggy moorlands, with some stretches of duckboard and flagstone path. Careful navigation is required in mist.
Refreshments	None.

Before leaving Byrness, ensure that you have a good weather forecast and enough food to get you through the Cheviot Hills, and if planning to move off-route in search of accommodation, it is essential to book in advance. After a steep, forested climb from Byrness, the moorland crest beyond has some bad boggy patches, though paths become firmer later. The Pennine Way passes the enormous Otterburn Ranges, which are surrounded by 'danger' notices. While some walkers leave Byrness very early to complete the whole distance to Kirk Yetholm in a day, others camp overnight at Clennell Street, head off-route to Uswayford for lodgings, or arrange a pick-up off-route at Cocklawfoot.

If starting from the youth hostel, walk towards the church, and cross over the road beforehand to pick up the path.

Start from the church in **Byrness**, and start walking towards the forestry village, but cross the A68 road and walk up a path rising from the road. ◄ The narrow tarmac path links with a tarmac drive. Walk down the drive, but quickly turn right as signposted for the Pennine Way, through a gap in a beech hedge. Keep to the right of a small field, going in and out of it using small gates. Climb straight up a path as marked, through bracken among tall conifers. Climb over a rise and drop down to a forest track. Cross over and climb up a bracken-clad forest ride and keep climbing to cross two more forest tracks.

The path is steep and is studded with boulders as it leaves the forest, scramble up a slope of bracken and bilberry, using hands to climb a low gritstone edge. Go through a gate where there may be a note about the Otterburn Ranges. ▶

Climb to the grassy moorland crest of **Byrness Hill**. There is a large cairn to the right, at 414m (1358ft), but the Pennine Way turns left along the grassy crest.

There are some squelchy spots along the crest, and bilberry grows among the grass in places. Climb a couple of short, steep slopes that have bouldery collars, on **Houx Hill** and **Windy Crag**, then follow a fence. Beware of a horrible bog where the fence turns slightly to the right, and if possible start to outflank it in advance. A firmer grassy path follows a fence onwards and downhill, on a slope bearing heather and bilberry. Cross a gap and climb uphill, reaching a cairn at 527m (1729ft) on **Ravens Knowe**. The path passes briefly behind a 'danger' sign, though there is nothing to worry about.

Walk down to a broad and boggy gap and pick up a long stretch of duckboard, avoiding black peat, tussocky grass, sphagnum moss and bog cotton. The duckboard ends and the fence crosses the grassy **Ogre Hill**, with forest to the left. Follow the fence and forest downhill, reaching a boggy valley at **Coquet Head**, where there is a junction of fences, a

Rest assured that at no point does the Pennine Way enter the military firing range.

Map continued on page 196

195

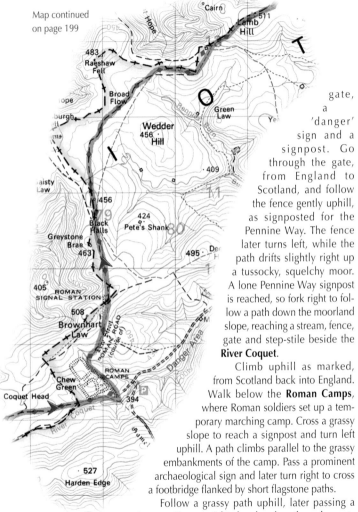

Map continued
on page 199

gate, a 'danger' sign and a signpost. Go through the gate, from England to Scotland, and follow the fence gently uphill, as signposted for the Pennine Way. The fence later turns left, while the path drifts slightly right up a tussocky, squelchy moor. A lone Pennine Way signpost is reached, so fork right to follow a path down the moorland slope, reaching a stream, fence, gate and step-stile beside the **River Coquet**.

Climb uphill as marked, from Scotland back into England. Walk below the **Roman Camps**, where Roman soldiers set up a temporary marching camp. Cross a grassy slope to reach a signpost and turn left uphill. A path climbs parallel to the grassy embankments of the camp. Pass a prominent archaeological sign and later turn right to cross a footbridge flanked by short flagstone paths.

Follow a grassy path uphill, later passing a signpost. Keep straight ahead and go through a gate in a fence. Pass another signpost and follow the path straight ahead, beside a fence, known as the 'border fence'. ▶ Follow the fence across a tussocky moorland, though looking over onto the Scottish side of the fence it is largely heather moorland. Reach a signpost at a gate on a kink in the fence at **Black Halls**, where the Roman road of Dere Street crosses.

This marks the border between England and Scotland, but keen map-readers will spot one tiny bit of Scotland lies on the 'English' side of the fence.

Keep to the right-hand side of the fence, and in fact, drift right away from it up a gentle slope of tussocky grass. The ground is boggy on the way up, but dry and grassy on top, where there is a marker post at 456m (1496ft). Walk gently downhill, crossing a dip and noticing more and more patches of heather on the moor. Flagstones appear on a broad and boggy dip, but more are needed. Pass a cairn on a firm patch of ground, then undulate across firm and boggy areas at **Broad Flow**, before following a short line of flagstones sinking into the bog. Cross another dip later and climb more steeply, becoming gentler on a hill at a fence corner. Follow the path directly to the **Yearning Saddle Hut**.

YEARNING SADDLE HUT

This purpose-built mountain refuge hut is located at 440m (1445ft), NT 804128, 14.5km (9 miles) from Byrness. It will serve more as a place to shelter for lunch than an emergency shelter for the night. On the other hand, anyone walking the Pennine Way north to south who has seriously underestimated their abilities after leaving Kirk Yetholm might well find themselves spending the night here. The next shelter on the Pennine Way is 21km (13 miles) ahead, or 18km (11 miles) if you omit The Cheviot.

Leave the hut and cross a dip, then follow the path uphill beside the fence. The tussocky grass gives way to heather towards the top. Pick up a flagstone path, passing close to a trig point at 511m (1677ft) on **Lamb Hill**. Walk down a heather slope to reach a broad gap. Follow the flagstone path across to the other side, then climb a peaty path on a heather slope. Another flagstone path continues

Following a broad and clear path along the crest of the Cheviot Hills towards Windy Gyle

onwards, bending right over a gentle rise and later climbing onto the top of **Beefstand Hill** at 562m (1844ft).

The flagstone path expires on the way downhill. Pass a gate and ladder stile where another fence joins the border fence. Continue along another flagstone path, down across a broad gap then up onto a hill to turn round a sharp left corner. Walk gently down onto a gap then follow a short, steep, peaty path to the top of **Mozie Law** at 552m (1811ft). Yet another flagstone path runs downhill, pulling away from the fence to cross a broad dip, returning to the fence later. A firm, grassy path runs downhill, though there is heather over the fence on the Scottish side. A gate and signpost are reached where a track is known simply as The Street, around 500m (1640ft).

Step over the track and head straight over a grassy moor. Cross a stream and cross a grassy hill, then walk down to a boggy dip. A short, steep climb leads back to the border fence and over a grassy rise. Either walk alongside the fence, or stay well to the right for a shortcut across the hillside. Walk down onto a grassy gap then follow the path and the fence up to a gate and stepstile. Cross to the Scottish side of the fence and climb up a slope of grass and bilberry. A huge cairn and a trig point stand on the summit of **Windy Gyle** at 619m (2031ft). ◀

Extensive views stretch well beyond the Cheviot Hills, into southern Scotland and back towards the North Pennines.

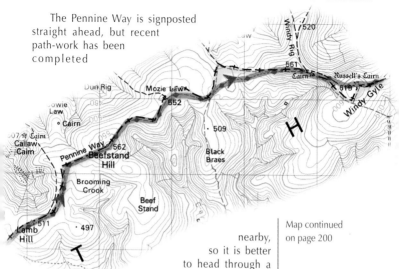

The Pennine Way is signposted straight ahead, but recent path-work has been completed

Map continued on page 200

nearby, so it is better to head through a gate in the nearby fence, back into England, then turn left and walk downhill. Pick up a flagstone path over boggy moorland, passing grass, heather, bilberry and bog cotton. The slabs end near the large **Russell's Cairn**, but once an adjoining fence has been crossed at a step-stile, more flagstones continue along a boggy, hummocky crest. The stone slabs alternate with a couple of stony stretches of path, then a gate and signpost are reached where the track known as **Clennell Street** crosses the broad moorland crest at 542m 1778ft).

Walkers who intend to continue to Kirk Yetholm, or at least to the next mountain refuge hut, should keep straight ahead along the Pennine Way. Those with camping gear can pitch nearby, but not on the track, in case a farmer needs to pass in a vehicle. The signpost beside the gate points right for Uswayford and left for Cocklawfoot. There is a remote farmhouse B&B at Uswayford, which must be booked in advance. Cocklawfoot is at a road-end where, by prior arrangement, a pick-up from Kirk Yetholm is possible.

Off-route to Uswayford

Walk away from the border fence on the English side. Follow a clear track down a heather moor. Pass through a gate in a fence, then when a signpost is reached, turn left and walk to another gate in a forest fence. Follow a path straight ahead, crossing a track to continue down a broad forest ride. Walk down to the bottom edge of the forest and turn right to follow **Usway Burn** downstream. Cross a footbridge and continue along the other bank of the burn to reach the farmhouse at **Uswayford**, at 360m (1180ft). Distance one-way: 2.5km (1½ miles).

Map continued from page 199

Off-route to Cocklawfoot

Go through the gate in the border fence to enter Scotland. Follow a track down a grass and heather moor, with a fence on the left-hand side. The track winds downhill and goes through a gate, then there is a gentle ascent. The stony surface gives way to grass and as the track descends it runs through a small forest, passing through a gate. Continue beside another small forest and drop down to a gate. The farm of **Cocklawfoot** is

on the right, but turn left to cross a metal bridge over a river, at 230m (755ft). A tarmac road continues and this is where accommodation providers from Kirk Yetholm will meet you. Distance one-way: 4km (2½ miles).

A long and winding track descends from Clennell Street to Cocklawfoot, where a pick-up is possible

DAY 20
Clennell Street to Kirk Yetholm

Start	Clennell Street, NY 871 160
Finish	The Green, Kirk Yetholm, NT 827 282
Distance	24km (15 miles)
Ascent	720m (2360ft); alternative 600m (1970ft)
Descent	1150m (3775ft); alternative 1030m (3380ft)
Maps	OS Landranger 74 and 80, OS Explorer OL16, Harvey's Pennine Way North
Terrain	Broad, high and exposed boggy moorlands, with some stretches of flagstone path and duckboard. Careful navigation is required in mist.
Refreshments	Pubs at Kirk Yetholm and nearby Town Yetholm.

The final day's walk on the Pennine Way is far from straightforward. Some walkers may have to return to the route from Uswayford or Cocklawfoot, or start from a high-level camp in the middle of the Cheviot Hills. Once the walk is underway, those who are running out of time or energy omit the spur route to The Cheviot. After passing The Schil, the final stage is wholly in Scotland, but there is still one more decision to be made. Originally, the Pennine Way headed straight down to Halterburn, but this quickly became an 'alternative' route. A new 'main' route was marked over an attractive range of hills. Either way, the route reaches its conclusion at Kirk Yetholm.

The first task, for those who moved off-route to Uswayford or Cocklawfoot, is to return to **Clennell Street**. The Pennine Way continues north-west along the border fence, following a flagstone path undulating gently down a crest of heather and bog cotton. Cross a ladder stile over an adjoining fence on a broad gap at **Butt Roads**, then climb a little until the flagstones finish. The path can be squelchy underfoot, then more flagstones pass a trig point at 531m (1742ft) on the way to **King's Seat**. Continue onwards and upwards past **Score Head** until the flagstones finish again.

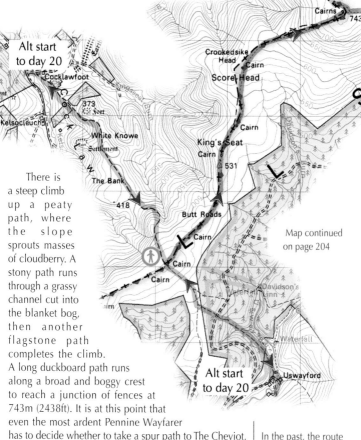

There is a steep climb up a peaty path, where the slope sprouts masses of cloudberry. A stony path runs through a grassy channel cut into the blanket bog, then another flagstone path completes the climb. A long duckboard path runs along a broad and boggy crest to reach a junction of fences at 743m (2438ft). It is at this point that even the most ardent Pennine Wayfarer has to decide whether to take a spur path to The Cheviot, 2.5km (1½ miles) distant, returning an hour or so later, or whether to turn left and head straight for Kirk Yetholm. Much depends on the weather, and how much time and stamina you have. ▶

Cross a step-stile over the fence, as signposted for the Cheviot Summit. Follow a flagstone path down among peat hags on a broad and boggy gap. Rise to the corner of a fence, where the flagstones finish. Walk up a grassy slope that can be wet and boggy, passing bog cotton and cloudberry. Either follow the fence or keep away from it,

In the past, the route to The Cheviot was a horribly boggy morass, but now there is a firm path most of the way there.

Map continued on page 204

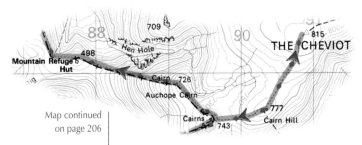

Map continued
on page 206

depending on conditions underfoot. Pass a signpost on the summit of **Cairn Hill** at 777m (2549ft), then walk down a firm, grassy slope beside the fence.

The plants on this boggy heather moorland slope are amazing, including great swathes of cloudberry, as well as bilberry, crowberry, bog cotton and tiny dwarf willows.

A flagstone path leads down to a broad and boggy gap, then climbs gently uphill. ◄ The path climbs and crosses two step-stiles while passing through a triangular fenced enclosure. Masses of cloudberry grow as the path levels out and reaches the summit of **The Cheviot** at 815m (2674ft). A stoutly buttressed trig point stands on a flagstone 'patio', where there was once a filthy, over-trodden peat bog. Unfortunately, this is not a good viewpoint because of the broadness of the summit plateau. Retrace your steps back to the junction of fences at 743m (2438ft) to continue the main route.

The stoutly buttressed trig point on the broad moorland top of The Cheviot at 815m (2674ft)

DANIEL DEFOE ON THE CHEVIOT

Daniel Defoe travelled extensively around Britain and was a little too enthusiastic when he compared British scenes with landscapes he had seen elsewhere in the world. The Cheviot was not immune from this 'over-interpretation' in 1726, when he compared it to El Teide on Tenerife, or imagined during the ascent that the summit would turn out to be a pinnacle! He wrote:

We were the more uneasy about, mounting highery [sic] because we all had a Notion, that when we came to the Top, we should be just as upon a Pinnacle, that the Hill narrowed to a Point, and we should have only Room enough to stand, with a Precipice every way round us; and with these Apprehensions, we all sat down upon the Ground, and said we would go no farther. Our Guide did not at first understand what we were apprehensive of; but at last by our Discourse he perceived the Mistake, and then not mocking our Fears, he told us, that indeed if it had been so, we had been in the Right, but he assur'd us, there was Room enough on the Top of the Hill to run a Race, if we thought fit, and we need not fear any thing of being blown off the Precipice, as we had suggested; so he Encouraging us we went on, and reach't the Top of the Hill in about half an Hour more.

Back at the junction of fences at 743m (2438ft), cross a step-stile and turn right to go through a gate. Follow a long duckboard path across a gentle boggy gap, climbing slightly onto the firm, grassy hump of **Auchope Cairn**, which bears two square-built cairns at 725m (2379ft). Drop down a steep and stony slope and follow a fence downhill on a grassy slope. Cross a gap and climb to a mountain refuge hut perched high above **Hen Hole**.

HEN HOLE HUT

This purpose-built mountain refuge hut (NT 879201) is located at almost 480m (1575ft), 13km (8 miles) from Kirk Yetholm. Most Pennine Wayfarers will poke their heads round the door, or use it briefly for shelter. A few, having overestimated their ability to walk all the way from Byrness to Kirk Yetholm in a day, may end up spending the night there.

Follow the path onwards to cross a gentle rise and a broad gap beyond, passing heather, bilberry and crowberry. There is a fine view along the College Valley. Walk over another broad and boggy hump bearing heather, bilberry and crowberry. A flagstone path crosses a boggy gap, but there are none leading uphill beside the border fence. Walk over a boggy hump and follow a flagstone path across a broad and boggy gap. Cross a step-stile over a fence beside a gate then climb a heathery slope, which becomes steep and grassy with patches of boulder-scree. Towards the top, cross the fence, if a slight detour appeals, to inspect the rocky peak and summit cairn on **The Schil**, at 601m (1972ft).

Follow the fence downhill onto a heathery slope. Join a tumbled drystone wall at a corner and follow it straight ahead across a squelchy bog. Cross a step-stile over a fence, beside a gate, then walk alongside the fence and wall onwards. Turn left to cross a ladder stile, passing from England to Scotland for the last time. Follow a grassy path on a gently rising traverse to a three-way signpost on a cairn below **Black Hag**. Left is signposted as the Pennine Way low-level alternative route, while right is signposted as the Pennine Way high-level main route.

Alternative route

This used to be the main route, but it suffered severe erosion and its use was discouraged. It is in good shape these days, and anyone suffering appalling weather on the Cheviot Hills will welcome the opportunity to use it. The path simply cuts across a grass and heather slope to reach a

Map continued on page 207

Black Hag
549

Hawthope Burn

601 The Schil

Birnie
Brae

87   88

498

Mountain Refuge
Hut

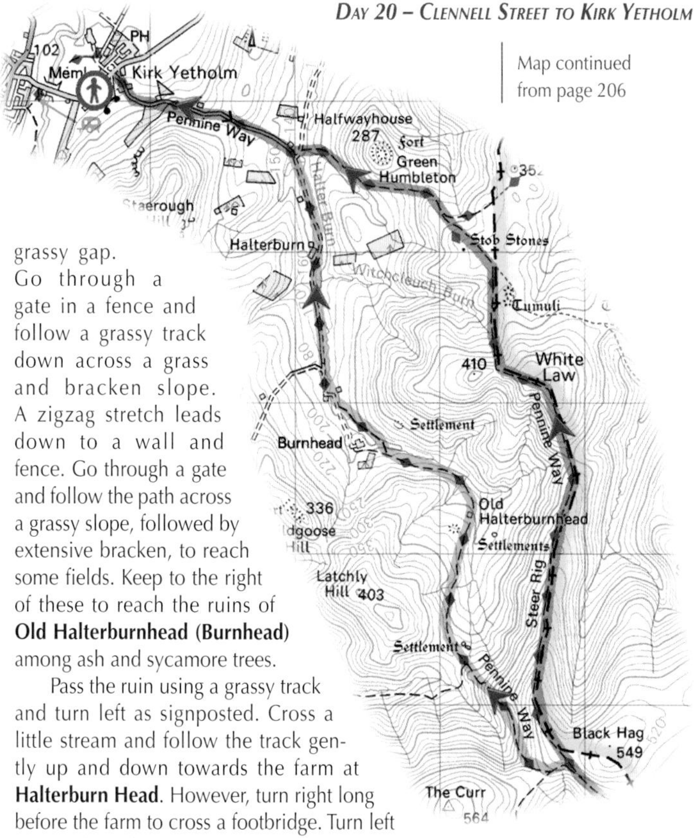

Map continued
from page 206

grassy gap.

Go through a gate in a fence and follow a grassy track down across a grass and bracken slope. A zigzag stretch leads down to a wall and fence. Go through a gate and follow the path across a grassy slope, followed by extensive bracken, to reach some fields. Keep to the right of these to reach the ruins of **Old Halterburnhead (Burnhead)** among ash and sycamore trees.

Pass the ruin using a grassy track and turn left as signposted. Cross a little stream and follow the track gently up and down towards the farm at **Halterburn Head**. However, turn right long before the farm to cross a footbridge. Turn left and go through a gate to walk beside a drystone wall and a fence. Turn left through another gate to join the farm access track, turning right to follow it to a cattle grid. Continue straight along a minor road and later pass buildings at **Halterburn**. Shortly afterwards, the main Pennine Way joins from the right.

Main route

The path leaves the three-way signpost and rises gently uphill. Go through a gate at a junction of fences on a grass and heather hump, enjoying views across a patchwork landscape of fields to the prominent three peaks of the Eildon Hills. Walk straight ahead, keeping to the left side of the border fence. The grassy crest runs downhill and passes a curious little outcrop of rock on **Steer Rigg**. When a junction of fences is reached, go through a gate and follow the fence further downhill to reach a grassy gap. Cross a little hump and pass a small outcrop, then walk further downhill to reach another grassy gap.

Climb straight up a steep and grassy slope, swinging left at the top and just missing the summit of **White Law**, at almost 430m (1410ft). Walk downhill beside the fence to reach a Pennine Way signpost beside gates and a ladder stile where the fence joins a drystone wall. Follow the wall downhill, then uphill a little, then veer left through bracken to pass a marker post. Walk up to another Pennine Way signpost and turn left to pick up a grassy track and follow it downhill. The next signpost is a combined one for the Pennine Way and St Cuthbert's Way. Keep walking downhill and keep right of a tin hut, following a narrow path across a slope of bracken. Walk down to a ford and footbridge over **Halter Burn** and cross to a road on the other side. The alternative route joins the main route at this point.

Turn right to climb steeply up the minor road, over a gap between low hills. There are benches beside the road for weary walkers, and journey's end can be seen ahead. The road leads straight down past a row of houses to reach a spacious green in the centre of **Kirk Yetholm**. The Border Hotel stands to the right, declaring itself 'The end of the Pennine Way'. Some walkers will check to see if the bar is open for a celebratory drink, while others will sit by the green and quietly reflect on the long journey that brought them here. All must consider, at some stage, how on earth they are going to get back home!

KIRK YETHOLM

This little village is very proud of its Gypsy heritage, and on the way down the High Street, walkers pass the 'Gypsy Palace', though it is only a little cottage. The two most notable Gypsy families were the Faas and the Marshalls.

Kirk Yetholm offers a small range of services, including the Border Hotel, a few B&Bs and a youth hostel. If any further services are required, a short walk leads to neighbouring Town Yetholm, where there is the Plough Hotel, a few B&Bs and a campsite, as well as a post office and shop. When the time comes to leave either village, there are occasional daily buses, except Sunday, heading for Kelso for onward bus connections, some leading direct to Berwick upon Tweed and Edinburgh, which have railway stations. On Sundays, the only service between Kirk Yetholm and Kelso is a Taxibus, which must be booked in advance.

The Border Hotel proclaims itself to be the 'end of the Pennine Way' in the village of Kirk Yetholm

209

APPENDIX A
Route summary table

The Pennine Way can be adapted to suit walkers of all abilities, and there is no particular need to follow the schedule outlined in this guidebook. Long days can be split. Short days can be extended. Pick-ups can be arranged wherever the route crosses a road, with careful planning. Nor is there any need to walk south to north, but this is the direction most people choose. Some do walk north to south. If you do this, you will need to reverse all the route directions, which could be a little confusing at times, but the signposting and waymarking seems to be as good in one direction as it is in the other. NB These statistics relate only to the main route, without any diversions off-route.

Day	Stage	Distance	Ascent	Descent
1	Edale to Crowden	29km (18 miles)	740m (2430ft)	780m (2560ft)
2	Crowden to Standedge	20km (12½ miles)	660m (2165ft)	480m (1575ft)
3	Standedge to Callis Bridge	26km (16 miles)	350m (1150ft)	640m (2100ft)
4	Callis Bridge to Ickornshaw	26km (16 miles)	880m (2885ft)	760m (2490ft)
5	Ickornshaw to Gargrave	19km (12 miles)	520m (1705ft)	600m (1970ft)
6	Gargrave to Malham	11km (7 miles)	200m (655ft)	100m (330ft)
7	Malham to Horton in Ribblesdale	24km (15 miles)	810m (2660ft)	780m (2560ft)
8	Horton in Ribblesdale to Hawes	24km (15 miles)	490m (1610ft)	490m (1610ft)
9	Hawes to Keld	21km (13 miles)	715m (2345ft)	615m (2020ft)
10	Keld to Baldersdale	24km (15 miles)	400m (1310ft)	400m (1310ft)

Day	Stage	Distance	Ascent	Descent
11	Baldersdale to Middleton-in-Teesdale	11km (7 miles)	300m (985ft)	400m (1310ft)
12	Middleton-in-Teesdale to Langdon Beck	14km (8½ miles)	230m (755ft)	80m (260ft)
13	Langdon Beck to Dufton	22km (13½ miles)	330m (1085ft)	530m (1740ft)
14	Dufton to Alston	32km (20 miles)	1040m (3410ft)	940m (3085ft)
15	Alston to Greenhead	27km (17 miles)	540m (1770ft)	700m (2295ft)
16	Greenhead to Housesteads	12km (7½ miles)	550m (1805ft)	450m (1475ft)
17	Housesteads to Bellingham	23km (14 miles)	380m (1245ft)	500m (1640ft)
18	Bellingham to Byrness	26km (16 miles)	550m (1805ft)	450m (1475ft)
19	Byrness to Clennell Street	23km (14 miles)	820m (2690ft)	500m (1640ft)
20	Clennell Street to Kirk Yetholm	24km (15 miles)	720m (2360ft)	1150m (3775ft)
Total		438km (272 miles)	11,225m (36,825ft)	11345m (37,220ft)

APPENDIX B
Useful contacts

PENNINE WAY
The Pennine Way has a national trail manager who ensures that the route remains free of obstructions, and that any damage occurring is repaired. The Pennine Way website is an excellent source of information about the route.

National Trail Manager – Pennine Way
Natural England
Bullring House
Wakefield
West Yorkshire
WF1 3BJ
Tel: 01924 334500
www.nationaltrail.co.uk/pennineway

The Pennine Way Association is a registered charity that exists to provide 'a focus of public interest' about the route. Membership is open to everyone and the association provides an accommodation list for the route.
www.penninewayassociation/co/uk

NATIONAL PARKS AND AONBS
The Pennine Way passes through three National Parks: the Peak District, Yorkshire Dales and Northumberland. It also passes through the South Pennines and the North Pennines Area of Outstanding Natural Beauty.

Peak District National Park Authority
Aldern House
Baslow Road
Bakewell
Derbyshire DE45 1AE
Tel:01629 816200
www.peakdistrict.org

Pennine Prospects (South Pennines)
Fourth Floor
Jacobs Well
Bradford
BD1 5RW
Tel: 01274 433536
South Pennines – www.pennineprospects.co.uk

Yorkshire Dales National Park Authority
Yoredale
Bainbridge
Leyburn
North Yorkshire
DL8 3EL
Tel: 0300 4560030
www.yorkshiredales.org.uk

North Pennines AONB Partnership
Weardale Business Centre
The Old Co-op Building
1 Martin Street
Stanhope
County Durham
DL13 2UY
Tel: 01388 528801
www.northpennines.org.uk

Northumberland National Park Authority
Eastburn
South Park
Hexham
Northumberland
NE46 1BS
Tel 01434 605555
www.northumberlandnationalpark.org.uk

TRANSPORT INFORMATION

Transport Direct provides impartial information for long-distance travel by car, train or coach –
www.transportdirect.info

Traveline is the best resource for checking local bus timetables – tel: 0871 2002233, www.traveline.org.uk

The National Taxi Hotline will put you in touch with the nearest taxi operator in the scheme – tel: 0800 645321.

TOURIST INFORMATION

Most towns and villages along the Pennine Way have tourist information centres, and these are mentioned throughout the route description. Use these places as the best source of local accommodation information. Most will be able to book lodgings on your behalf, saving you the expense and hassle of phoning. They also hold details of local attractions and events, as well as timetables for local bus and rail services. Some have detailed town or village plans, maps, guidebooks, local crafts and souvenirs for sale. Several lie on or close to the Pennine Way:

Edale
Tel: 01629 816587
Saddleworth
Tel: 01457 870336
Marsden
Tel: 01484 845595
Rochdale
Tel: 01706 864928
Hebden Bridge
Tel: 01422 843832
Haworth
Tel: 01535 642329
Malham
Tel: 01729 830673
Horton in Ribblesdale
Tel: 01729 860333

Hawes
Tel: 01969 667450
Middleton-in-Teesdale
Tel: 01833 641001
Appleby
Tel: 017683 51177
Alston
Tel: 01434 382244
Haltwhistle
Tel: 01434 322002
Bellingham
Tel: 01434 220616
Kelso
Tel: 01573 223464

BAGGAGE TRANSFER

Baggage transfer companies operate along the Pennine Way. Using them can be expensive, especially at the northern end of the route, but many walkers are willing to pay the price for a comfortable walk.

Brigantes Walking Holidays
Rookery Cottage
Kirkby Malham
Skipton
BD23 4BX
Tel: 01729 830463
www.brigantesenglishwalks.com

Complete packages organised for the Pennine Way, including accommodation and baggage transfer.

Discovery Travel Holidays
Opsa House
5a High Ousegate
York
YO1 8ZZ
Tel: 01904 632226
www.discoverytravel.co.uk

Complete packages organised for the Pennine Way, including accommodation and baggage transfer.

The Sherpa Van
29 The Green
Richmond
North Yorkshire
DL10 4RG
Tel: 0871 5200124
www.sherpavan.com

Pennine Way accommodation and baggage transfer organised between Malham and Kirk Yetholm.

HUMOUR

It's easy to get too serious about the Pennine Way. The following books are recommended to lighten the mood:

One Man and his Bog, by Barry Pilton, published by Corgi.

Pennine Walkies, by Mark Wallington, published by Arrow.

APPENDIX C
Facilities along the route

Day	Location (ends of stages shown in bold)	Distance from day start	Distance from route start	Guest house/ B&B	Hostel	Campsite	Pub/ café	Shop	ATM
	Edale	0km (0 miles)	0km (0 miles)	✓	✓ off-route	✓	✓	✓	
Day 1	**Crowden**	29km (18 miles)	29km (18 miles)	✓ off-route		✓	✓	✓ basic	
	Wessenden Head	13km (8 miles)	42km (26 miles)				✓ snack van		
	Marsden (off-route)			✓			✓	✓	
Day 2	**Standedge**	20km (12½miles)	49km (30½ miles)	✓ off-route		✓ off-route	✓ off-route	✓	
	Diggle (off-route)			✓					
	Bleakedgate	7km (4½ miles)	56km (35 miles)				✓ snack van		
	White House	12km (7½ miles)	61km (38 miles)		✓		✓		
	Mankinholes (off-route)			✓	✓	✓	✓		
	Hebden Bridge (off-route)			✓			✓	✓	✓
Day 3	**Callis Bridge**	26km (16 miles)	75km (46½ miles)	✓					
	Blackshaw Head	2.5km (1½ miles)	77.5km (48 miles)	✓		✓	✓		
	Jack Bridge (off-route)						✓ basic café		
	Colden	3km (2 miles)	78km (48½ miles)			✓		✓	
	Blake Dean (off route)						✓		

Day	Location (ends of stages shown in bold)	Distance from day start	Distance from route start	Guest house/ B&B	Hostel	Campsite	Pub/ café	Shop	ATM
	Haworth (off-route)								
	Ponden	18km (11 miles)	93km (57½ miles)	✓	✓		✓	✓	✓
Day 4	**Ickornshaw**	26km (16 miles)	101km (62½ miles)	✓				✓	
	Lothersdale	5km (3 miles)	106km (65½ miles)	✓		✓	✓	✓	
	East Marton	14km (9 miles)	115km (71½ miles)			✓	✓	✓	
	Newton Grange (off-route)			✓					
Day 5	**Gargrave**	19km (12 miles)	120km (74½ miles)	✓		✓	✓	✓	✓
	Airton	6km (4 miles)	126km (78½ miles)				✓	✓	
	Kirkby Malham (off-route)						✓		
Day 6	**Malham**	11km (7 miles)	131km (81½ miles)	✓	✓	✓	✓	✓	
Day 7	**Horton in Ribblesdale**	24km (15 miles)	155km (96½ miles)	✓	✓	✓	✓	✓	
Day 8	**Hawes**	24km (15 miles)	179km (111½ miles)	✓		✓	✓	✓	
	Hardraw	2.5km (1½ miles)	181.5km (113 miles)	✓		✓	✓		
	Thwaite	16km (10 miles)	195km (121½ miles)	✓			✓		
Day 9	**Keld**	21km (13 miles)	200km (124½ miles)	✓		✓	✓	✓	
	Tan Hill Inn	6.5km (4 miles)	206.5km (128½ miles)	✓			✓		

Day	Location (ends of stages shown in bold)	Distance from day start	Distance from route start	Guest house/ B&B	Hostel	Campsite	Pub/ café	Shop	ATM
	Tan Hill Inn	6.5km (4 miles)	206.5km (128½ miles)	✓			✓		
Day 10	**Baldersdale**	24km (15miles)	224km (139½ miles)	✓					
	Bowes			✓		✓	✓	✓	✓
Day 11	**Middleton-in-Teesdale**	11km (7 miles)	235km (146½ miles)	✓		✓	✓	✓	✓
	Bowlees (off-route)						✓		
Day 12	**Langdon Beck**	14km (8½ miles)	249km (155 miles)	✓	✓	✓		✓ at hostel	
Day 13	**Dufton**	22km (13½ miles)	271km (168½ miles)	✓	✓	✓	✓	✓	✓
	Garrigill	26.5km (16½ miles)	297.5km (185 miles)	✓		✓ basic	✓	✓	
Day 14	**Alston**	32km (20 miles)	303km (188½ miles)	✓	✓	✓	✓	✓	✓
	Kirkhaugh	5km (3 miles)	308km (191½ miles)				✓ rarely		
	Slaggyford	10km (6 miles)	313km (194½ miles)	✓					
	Knarsdale (off-route)						✓		
Day 15	**Greenhead**	27km (17 miles)	330km (205½ miles)	✓		✓	✓	✓	
	Walltown	2.5km (1½ miles)	332.5km (207 miles)	✓			✓	basic	

Day	Location (ends of stages shown in bold)	Distance from day start	Distance from route start	Guest house/ B&B	Hostel	Campsite	Pub/ café	Shop	ATM
	Cawfields	8km (5 miles)	338km (210½ miles)				✔ off-route		
	Twice Brewed (off route)			✔	✔	✔	✔		
Day 16	**Housesteads**	12km (7½ miles)	342km (213 miles)	✔ off-route					
Day 17	**Bellingham**	23km (14 miles)	365km (227 miles)	✔	✔	✔	✔	✔	✔
Day 18	**Byrness**	26km (16 miles)	391km (243 miles)	✔	✔	✔	✔	✔	
Day 19	**Clennell Street**	23km (14 miles)	414km (257 miles)						
	Uswayford (off-route)			✔					
Day 20	**Kirk Yetholm**	24km (15 miles)	438km (272 miles)	✔	✔	✔	✔	✔ off-route	

LISTING OF CICERONE GUIDES

Across the Eastern Alps: E5
Walking in the Alps
Tour of the Matterhorn
100 Hut Walks in the Alps
Alpine Points of View
Tour of Monte Rosa
Snowshoeing
Alpine Ski Mountaineering
    Vol 1: Western Alps
    Vol 2: Central and Eastern Alps

FRANCE
Mont Blanc Walks
Tour of the Vanoise
Tour of the Oisans: The GR54
The GR5 Trail
Walking in the Languedoc
Écrins National Park
The Robert Louis Stevenson Trail
Tour of the Queyras
The Cathar Way
GR20: Corsica
Trekking in the Vosges and Jura
Walking in the Cathar Region
Walking in the Dordogne
Mont Blanc Walks
Walking in the Haute Savoie
    North
    South
Walking on Corsica
Walking in Provence
Vanoise Ski Touring
Walking in the Cevennes
Walking in the Tarentaise &
    Beaufortain Alps
Walking the French Gorges
Walks in Volcano Country

PYRENEES AND FRANCE/SPAIN CROSS-BORDER ROUTES
The Pyrenean Haute Route
Through the Spanish Pyrenees: GR11
Walks and Climbs in the Pyrenees
The Mountains of Andorra
Way of St James
    France
    Spain
The GR10 Trail
Rock Climbs In The Pyrenees

SPAIN & PORTUGAL
Walking in Madeira
Walking the GR7 in Andalucia
Trekking through Mallorca
Walking in Mallorca
Via de la Plata
Walking in the Algarve
Walking in the Sierra Nevada
Walking in the Canary Islands
    Vol 2 East
Walking in the Cordillera Cantabrica
Costa Blanca Walks
    Vol 1 West
    Vol 2 East
The Mountains of Central Spain
Walks and Climbs in the Picos de
    Europa

SWITZERLAND
Tour of the Jungfrau Region
The Bernese Alps

Walks in the Engadine
Alpine Pass Route
Walking in the Valais
Walking in Ticino

GERMANY
Walking in the Bavarian Alps
Walking the River Rhine Trail
Germany's Romantic Road
Walking in the Harz Mountains
Walking in the Salzkammergut
King Ludwig Way

EASTERN EUROPE
Walking in Bulgaria's National Parks
The High Tatras
Walking in Hungary
The Mountains of Romania

SCANDINAVIA
Walking in Norway

SLOVENIA, CROATIA AND MONTENEGRO
Trekking in Slovenia
The Mountains of Montenegro
The Julian Alps of Slovenia

ITALY
Via Ferratas of the Italian Dolomites
    Vols 1 & 2
Italy's Sibillini National Park
Gran Paradiso
Walking in Tuscany
Through the Italian Alps
Trekking in the Apennines
Walking in Sicily
Walking in the Dolomites
Treks in the Dolomites
Shorter Walks in the Dolomites
Central Apennines of Italy
Walking in the Central Italian Alps
Italian Rock

MEDITERRANEAN
The High Mountains of Crete
Jordan: Walks, Treks, Caves, Climbs
    and Canyons
The Mountains of Greece
Walking in Malta
Western Crete
Treks & Climbs in Wadi Rum, Jordan
The Ala Dag

HIMALAYA
Bhutan
The Mount Kailash Trek
Everest: A Trekker's Guide
Annapurna: A Trekker's Guide
Manaslu: A Trekker's Guide
Kangchenjunga: A Trekker's Guide
Garhwal & Kumaon: A Trekker's and
    Visitor's Guide
Langtang with Gosainkund &
    Helambu: A Trekker's Guide

NORTH AMERICA
The Grand Canyon
British Columbia

SOUTH AMERICA
Aconcagua and the Southern Andes

AFRICA
Walking in the Drakensberg
Trekking in the Atlas Mountains

Kilimanjaro: A Complete Trekker's
    Guide
Climbing in the Moroccan Anti-Atlas

IRELAND
The Irish Coast To Coast Walk
Irish Coastal Walks
The Mountains Of Ireland

EUROPEAN CYCLING
The Grand Traverse of the Massif
    Central
Cycle Touring in Ireland
Cycling the Canal du Midi
Cycling in the French Alps
Cycle Touring in Switzerland
The Way of St James
Cycle Touring in France
Cycling the River Loire
Cycle Touring in Spain
The Danube Cycleway

INTERNATIONAL CHALLENGES, COLLECTIONS AND ACTIVITIES
Europe's High Points
Canyoning

AUSTRIA
Trekking in Austria's Hohe Tauern
Walking in Austria
Trekking in the Zillertal Alps
Trekking in the Stubai Alps
Klettersteig: Scrambles in the
    Northern Limestone Alps

TECHNIQUES
Indoor Climbing
The Book of the Bivvy
Moveable Feasts
Rock Climbing
Sport Climbing
Mountain Weather
Map and Compass
The Hillwalker's Guide to
    Mountaineering
Outdoor Photography
The Hillwalker's Manual
Beyond Adventure
Snow and Ice Techniques

MINI GUIDES
Pocket First Aid and Wilderness
    Medicine
Navigating with a GPS
Navigation
Snow
Avalanche!

For full and up-to-date information
on our ever-expanding list of guides,
please visit our website:
www.cicerone.co.uk.

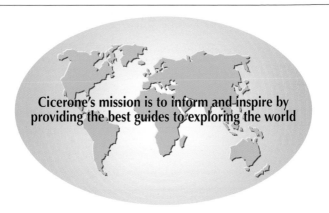

Cicerone's mission is to inform and inspire by providing the best guides to exploring the world

Since its foundation 40 years ago, Cicerone has specialised in publishing guidebooks and has built a reputation for quality and reliability. It now publishes nearly 300 guides to the major destinations for outdoor enthusiasts, including Europe, UK and the rest of the world.

Written by leading and committed specialists, Cicerone guides are recognised as the most authoritative. They are full of information, maps and illustrations so that the user can plan and complete a successful and safe trip or expedition – be it a long face climb, a walk over Lakeland fells, an alpine cycling tour, a Himalayan trek or a ramble in the countryside.

With a thorough introduction to assist planning, clear diagrams, maps and colour photographs to illustrate the terrain and route, and accurate and detailed text, Cicerone guides are designed for ease of use and access to the information.

If the facts on the ground change, or there is any aspect of a guide that you think we can improve, we are always delighted to hear from you.

Cicerone Press
2 Police Square Milnthorpe Cumbria LA7 7PY
Tel: 015395 62069 Fax: 015395 63417
info@cicerone.co.uk www.cicerone.co.uk

CICERONE